HARTLEY COLERIDGE

NEW POEMS

HARTLEY COLERIDGE
A few years before his death.
(From a portrait by M.ʳ Tyson)

HARTLEY COLERIDGE

NEW POEMS

INCLUDING A SELECTION
FROM HIS PUBLISHED POETRY

Edited by

EARL LESLIE GRIGGS

GREENWOOD PRESS, PUBLISHERS
WESTPORT, CONNECTICUT

The Library of Congress has catalogued this publication as follows:

Library of Congress Cataloging in Publication Data

Coleridge, Hartley, 1796-1849.
    New poems.

    CONTENTS: Poems published by Hartley Coleridge in
1833.--Posthumous poems published by Derwent Coleridge
in 1851.--Unpublished and uncollected poems.
PR4467.A2G7 1972   821'.7   73-136059
ISBN 0-8371-5209-7

79737

Originally published in 1942
by Oxford University Press, London

Reprinted with the permission
of Oxford University Press

Reprinted from an original copy in the collections
of the Brooklyn Public Library

First Greenwood Reprinting 1972

Library of Congress Catalogue Card Number 73-136059

ISBN 0-8371-5209-7

Printed in the United States of America

TO

EDMUND BLUNDEN

A MODERN ENGLISH POET WHO WILL READ THESE
POEMS WITH SYMPATHETIC INSIGHT
AND UNDERSTANDING, THIS
VOLUME IS DEDICATED

PREFACE

'But *thou*, my babe!' wrote Samuel Taylor Coleridge of little Hartley,

> shalt wander like a breeze
> By lakes and sandy shores, beneath the crags
> Of ancient mountain, and beneath the clouds,
> Which image in their bulk both lakes and shores
> And mountain crags:

and listening to the nightingale, he promised

> if that Heaven
> Should give me life, his childhood shall grow up
> Familiar with these songs, that with the night
> He may associate joy.

And so, indeed, Hartley did grow up. Wordsworth, too, poured out his affection in the lines *To H. C. Six Years Old:*

> O blessed vision! happy child!
> Thou art so exquisitely wild,
> I think of thee with many fears
> For what may be thy lot in future years.
>
> I thought of times when Pain might be thy guest,
> Lord of thy house and hospitality;
> And Grief, uneasy lover! never rest
> But when she sate within the touch of thee.
> O too industrious folly!
> O vain and causeless melancholy!
> Nature will either end thee quite;
> Or, lengthening out thy season of delight,
> Preserve for thee, by individual right,
> A young lamb's heart among the full-grown flocks.

Thus cherished and beloved in his childhood, Hartley Coleridge grew to maturity without learning a sense of responsibility, and he tended more and more to escape from reality into the dream world of his imagination. But if his existence became aimless— a scholar gipsy Edmund Blunden appropriately called him—he never forfeited the love of his fellow men, and except for an irresistible craving for drink and a congenital weakness of will, he was innocent and blameless. Exiled in young manhood to the Lake Country, after having been dismissed at the end of his probationary year as Fellow of Oriel College and after having proved utterly unable to support himself in London, he became neither morose nor sullen, but overflowed with a genuine love for humanity, particularly for men and women in the humblest walks of life. Something in his sweet and unassuming nature awakened the protective instinct in those about him. Everyone loved him, and as the years wore on, he became the charge of the whole countryside. Instead of condemning or shunning him, everybody, from Wordsworth to the most simple-hearted dalesman, regarded him with feelings of love and pity. Samuel Taylor Coleridge, who grieved bitterly over his son's instability, wrote with remarkable understanding of Hartley only a few years before his own death:

'Poor dear Hartley! He was hardly—nay, cruelly—used by the Oriel men—and it fell with a more crushing weight on him, that with all his defects Love had followed him like his shadow and still does. If you can conceive, in connection with an excellent heart, sound religious principles, a mind constitutionally religious, and lastly, an active and powerful Intellect—if you can conceive, I say, in connection with all these, not a *mania*, not a *derangement*, but an *ideocy* of Will or rather of Volition, you will have formed a tolerably correct conception of Hartley Coleridge. Wordsworth says—I lament it but have ceased to condemn him. All this I have written in *confidence*. What Queen Mary said, on the loss of our last stronghold in France, that if her Heart were opened, Calais would be found at the core, I may say of my poor dear Hartley. I can never read Wordsworth's delightful lines to "H. C. at six years old"—without a feeling of awe, blended with tenderer emotions—so prophetic were they!'

For his part Hartley loved everything about him—the mountains and the lakes, the flowers and the birds, and his acquaintances, young and old. No wedding, christening, or even funeral was complete without him. In the solitude of his study he indulged in bitter self-condemnation for a life misspent; but when in company he was usually gay and looked on the world in Christian charity. Posterity has, perhaps, passed a fairer and a kinder judgment on Hartley Coleridge than he himself could do; and we can all agree with Aubrey de Vere that he might 'have been more easily changed into an angel than into a simply strong man.'

The charm of Hartley Coleridge's poetry lies in its intimate, personal nature. Brought up under the tutelage of Coleridge, Southey, and Wordsworth, he reflects mostly the influence of the last. While he possesses something of Southey's jesting anti-quarianism (and Charles Lamb's quaint humour as well), and while he inherited his father's passion for nature's particular hues and forms—the last leaf hanging to the oak or the restless aspen swaying in the breeze—he sees something of the spiritual harmony of the world and feels the 'presence that disturbs' him 'with the joy of elevated thoughts.' But for Wordsworth's sublime subjectivity Hartley Coleridge substitutes a warm personal feeling. Wordsworth loved his fellow-men, but he brooded over human misery without fully sharing it. He heard, indeed, 'the still, sad music of humanity,' but unlike Prince Hal he did not sound 'the very base-string of humility.' Hartley Coleridge, on the contrary, was a partaker of life's smiles and tears. His love of humanity lay at the very roots of his being. Wordsworth stood aloof, and every conversation with a child (as witness *We Are Seven*) came from conscious effort. Hartley Coleridge frequented the taverns, visited the dalesmen, laughed with the children, and lived on a plane of equality with his associates. Wordsworth *asked* the child questions; Hartley danced with her on the green. That is why, twenty years after both poets were dead, Canon Rawnsley, going over the Lake Country in search of anecdotes about Wordsworth, was amus-ingly surprised to hear that the elder poet was 'nowt to li'le Hartley. Li'le Hartley was a philosopher, you see; Wudsworth was a poet. Ter'ble girt difference betwixt them two ways, ye kna.' Indeed, the persons whom Canon Rawnsley consulted, understood both poets pretty well. 'But as fur Mister Wuds-worth, he'd pass you, same as if ya was nobbut a stoan. He niver cared for children, however; ya may be certain of that, for didn't I have to pass him four times in t' week, up to the door wi' meat? And he niver oncst said owt.' Unlike Hartley, he 'was niver a frequenter of public houses, or owt of that sort.' There was the story, too, that 'Hartley helped him [Wordsworth] a deal, . . . did best part of his poems for him, so the sayin' is.' Dislike, or at best a sense of awe, kept the dalesmen from Wordsworth. 'You could tell fra the man's faace his potry would niver have no laugh in it. His potry was quite different work from li'le Hartley. Hartley 'ud goa running along beside o' the brooks and mak his, and goa in the first oppen door and write what he had got upo' paper. But Wudsworth's potry was real hard stuff, and bided a deal of makking, and he'd keep it

in his head for long enough.' And so it was, as one dalesman
said, that although 'folks goes a deal to see where he's interred;
. . . for my part I'd walk twice distance over Fells to see where
Hartley lies.'

Thus, in the poems of Hartley Coleridge we find intimate self-
revelation and a tender love of little things. The highest
achievements of genius lay outside his abilities; but he is un-
excelled in 'the spontaneous overflow of powerful feelings.'
Through this poems we see into his character. They show his
pathetic self-condemnation, his realization of blasted hopes and
aspirations, his wistful yearning for feminine companionship,
and his tragic sense of change; but they also reveal him in his
gayer moods—when he refuses to bend in homage to his 'lofty'
kinswoman, when he scribbles his poetic impressions of a merry
excursion on the walls of a farmhouse, when he soliloquises over
his pet cat, or when he pauses to laugh at the laureateship or to
burlesque Wordsworth. Humour and pathos mingle closely in
his poems. We find impromptu verses on births, deaths, and
marriages, tributes to his father, and songs of the weather. But
gay or sad, lonely or in company, Hartley Coleridge dwelt with
what was nearest and dearest to him. He is the poet of the
simple joys of country folk, of 'the merry month of May' and
grim November, and of the hopes and fears of daily life. He
wrote most exquisitely of childhood—of the babe in the cradle,
of the young boy on the verge of maturity, and of the sweet
innocence of young girls. He was, indeed, as someone has said,
the laureate to countless baby boys and 'wee ladies sweet.' At
his best he possessed rare powers of expression, and he wrote
of his daily life with refreshing simplicity. Others have written
more profoundly than he, but for no poet has verse been a more
direct and spontaneous vehicle for moods, fancies, and conscience
than for him.

Though occasionally Hartley Coleridge gives evidence of
careful revision, he seems to have been an impatient writer.
All too frequently a poem begins in a promising manner but
weakens towards the, end. The inspiration came in a happy
phrase or line, only to flag before the poem was finished. Some-
times the demands of rhyme and measure proved insuperable
and a mere fragment remains; at other times he forced a con-
clusion, resting satisfied with inferior craftsmanship. Occasion-
ally he examined his work with a critical eye; hence he added
such comments as 'worth hammering at,' though he seldom did

so. That he recognized his limitations the following quotation from an unpublished notebook shows:

'I would fain produce something worthy of my father's son —but I fear—I almost fear the day is gone past. I have certainly lost much of my confidence in my own powers. I know not whether I possess the constructive faculty. Invention of a certain sort, I do not lack. I could string [together] incidents, and portray characters in prose or verse with sufficient facility, but I cannot foresee. Of all my verses, not a single copy was begun with any definite purpose. In every sonnet the idea has come upon me in the course of composition—sometimes it may be suggested by a rhyme—and yet if my own judgement be trustworthy, they are not deficient in singleness or completeness.'

Composition for Hartley Coleridge was, then, a means of self-expression, and his poems, as someone once said, 'carry about them an air of improvisation.' His ideas and feelings simply flowed into his pen. 'He never kneaded,' wrote Thomas Blackburne to Derwent Coleridge, 'or pounded his thoughts; they always came out *cap-à-pie*, like a troop in quick march. To see him brandishing his pen . . . and now and then beating time with his foot, and breaking out into a shout at any felicitous idea, was a thing never to be forgotten.' Since he depended so much on the inspiration of the moment, his chief excellence lies in single lines, in brief passages, or in short poems, and he gives almost no examples of sustained poetic power.

The sonnet, indeed, was his forte, and upon it must rest his reputation as a poet. It apparently imposed exactly the technical challenge he needed, and it suited perfectly his subjective manner. In his more introspective moods his sonnets reveal a tortured conscience, a sense of frustration, a kinship with Wordsworth's thorn, 'alone, bare and barren and blasted, ill-omen'd and unsightly;' but in other moods they sing of nature in her changing colours, of friends in joy or sorrow, of Sabbath evenings and the roadside chapel. Distinguished by technical excellence, often arresting in the harmonious blending of idea and expression, and memorable in their direct simplicity, his sonnets are living monuments of self-portraiture. They are unexcelled in quiet beauty, and Samuel Waddington was probably right in declaring that 'after Shakespeare our *sweetest* English sonneteer is Hartley Coleridge.'

.   .   .   .   .

From the time of the publication of his *Poems* in 1833, Hartley Coleridge intended to issue additional volumes of verse, but he never succeeded in doing so. Though he occasionally contributed poems to magazines, on his death in 1849 he left behind him a large body of unpublished poetry. In 1851, Derwent Coleridge, who with his sister inherited his brother's literary remains, published two volumes of Hartley Coleridge's poetry, the first volume including a Memoir and the poems of 1833, the second and larger volume containing posthumous poems. In 1908, Ramsay Colles reprinted Derwent Coleridge's edition in the Muses Library, omitting the Memoir and adding four or five new poems. Since 1908 no edition of Hartley Coleridge has been published. Interest in the poet has not waned, however. Examples of his poetry nearly always appear in Nineteenth Century anthologies, and he has been the subject of several recent studies.

The present editor, delving among the Hartley Coleridge papers in the possession of the Rev. G. H. B. Coleridge, came across nearly three hundred unpublished poems, many of them in the poet's own handwriting. A further search revealed the existence of a number of manuscripts in private hands or public libraries, and these materials were generously made available. The present edition, therefore, is a selection from both the unpublished and published poetry of Hartley Coleridge, and every effort has been made to choose those poems most representative of the poet's genius.

The unpublished poems are richer in autobiographical materials than those previously published, and they contain innumerable examples of Hartley Coleridge's wit and humour. Derwent Coleridge held himself to a pretty strict editorial policy, and 'more than half of the poems found in manuscript' were laid aside. 'No piece,' he writes, 'has been admitted of pure drollery, or in which the occasional character appeared to predominate; although many of these *jeux d'esprit*—outpourings of a sportive fancy, and of a most affectionate heart—gave much pleasure in the author's immediate circle, and are such, perhaps, as none but himself could have produced.' The present editor believes that many of these pieces are worth rescuing from oblivion.

For convenience the present volume is divided into three sections. The first part contains a selection from the poems published by Hartley Coleridge himself in 1833; the second division contains poems selected from the posthumous volume of 1851; and the third section includes poems hitherto

unpublished or published only in fugitive sources. Only
one of the longer poems (*Ada of Grasmere*) has been inclu-
ded. Hartley Coleridge was not at his best in long poems; his
genius seems to have become restless under sustained
effort. His *Prometheus*, his most ambitious attempt, is un-
finished; his *Leonard and Susan* is somewhat sentimental and
though Wordsworthian never rises to poetic power; *Mince Pie*
and *The Tea-table*, both of which appeared in magazines,
show an easy command of the heroic couplet and a pleasant
play of fancy, but neither is distinguished. *Ada of Grasmere*,
however, is of cons derable interest. While Hartley Coleridge
used the theme of Bürger's *Leonore* and endeavoured to imitate
the metre and manner of his father's *Christabel*, he succeeded
in producing a delightful poem.

Inasmuch as the present edition represents a selection from
the poems of Hartley Coleridge, no attempt to offer variant
readings has been made. In the first group of poems (those
selected from the poet's own volume of 1833) the changes in
spelling and punctuation made in the interests of clarity by
Derwent Coleridge in 1851 have been adopted. In the second
group of poems (those taken from Derwent Coleridge's second
volume of 1851) the present editor has been able in many cases
to collate the text with Hartley Coleridge's own manuscripts.
Derwent Coleridge's improvements in spelling and punctuation
have been retained, for the poet was often too eccentric in such
matters; but where the manuscript has been misread, as occasion-
ally happened with words or phrases, or where a better or
revised version existed in manuscript, the proper emendations
have been substituted. Important changes occur in the following
poems in this group:

IV (*On My Twin Niece and Nephew*); XVI (*To Mrs. Charles
Fox*)
    XIX ('How strange the cold ungenial atmosphere')
    XXI (*On a Calm Day towards the Close of the Year*)
    XXII (*Christmas Day*); XXIII (*December*, 1838)
    XXIV (*To a Snow-drop*); XXIX (*The God-child*)
    XXXIII (*Written on the 29th of May* 1847); XLI (*Privileges*)
    XLIII (*To a Friend*); XLVII (*To —— —— —— —*)
    LII (*The Fourth Birthday*); LIV (*The Anemone*)
    LVI ('Who would have thought, upon this icy cliff,')
    LVIII (*Wytheburn Chapel and Hostel*).
In the third group of poems (most of which are now published
for the first time) every effort has been made to follow Hartley
Coleridge's text exactly, but certain changes in spelling and

punctuation have been made in the interests of clarity, because many of the poems were written in great haste and because the text in some cases is from transcripts. Hartley Coleridge was excessively fond of the dash, using it instead of the comma, the semicolon, and the full-stop, and occasionally merely to mark the end of a line. Wherever the dash does not interfere with the reader's understanding, it has been retained, even though its superfluous use often gives the effect of carelessness and haste.

In each of the three parts of this volume the sonnets have been placed first, but it has seemed unwise to follow Derwent Coleridge's rather ingenious subject headings. The present editor has undertaken, however, to group together poems of the same mood or theme. Titles are given only when they appeared on the original manuscripts or when they were supplied by earlier transcribers. Footnotes indicating the whereabouts of manuscripts not belonging to the Coleridge family have been appended, and certain biographical, introductory, or explanatory comments (usually from Hartley Coleridge's own notebooks and letters) have been included.

In his efforts to collect his brother's poems Derwent Coleridge in general met with the most cordial response, and a good many manuscripts were sent to him for transcription. Joseph Burns, one of Hartley's acquaintances living at Hawkshead, however, was not so obliging. Burns claimed that Hartley had written certain poems for him in repayment for hospitality, and without consulting the Coleridge family he approached Edward Moxon and Longman about issuing these poems. The publishers got in touch with Derwent Coleridge, who took steps to prevent publication. Burns became cantankerous, wrote a series of highly insulting letters, and threatened to publish in spite of protests. In Burns's collection was Hartley's parody of *Peter Bell*, and Derwent, who had not seen the poem and had reason to fear it might prove offensive to the ageing Wordsworth, was particularly anxious that it should not appear. After having recourse to legal advice, Derwent induced Burns to turn over to him for a sum of twenty guineas the collection of poems and a rather naïve and childish memoir.

.   .   .   .   .

I am again indebted to the Rev. G. H. B. Coleridge for permission to use the manuscripts in his possession. It is a pleasure to express the deep sense of obligation which I, in common with all Coleridgean students, owe to Mr. Coleridge for his courtesy, liberality, and helpfulness.

I gratefully acknowledge a grant made by the Committee of the Faculty Research Fund of the University of Michigan, to aid me in the preparation of this volume. I wish also to acknowledge the personal interest and encouragement of Dr. Clarence S. Yoakum, Dean of the Horace H. Rackham School of Graduate Studies of the University of Michigan.

I am indebted for copies of Hartley Coleridge's poems and for permission to use them to Mr. J. K. Hudson, Sir S. H. Scott, Bart., Mr. Davidson Cook, Mr. Herbert Bell, Mr. Charles H. Godfrey, Mr. T. P. Godfrey, the Rev. C. H. Steel, Miss E. Hudson, Mr. Eric Flawn, Mr. J. A. Walmsley, Mr. M. A. Swinburn, Professor H. W. Garrod, Mrs. Ada Gawthrop Tertis, Mr. F. H. Clay and the Rev. Canon R. Quirk (Trustees of the Rev. J. H. Clay), and Miss N. I. Clay. Mr. J. K. Hudson, Mr. C. H. Godfrey, and Mr. T. P. Godfrey were especially helpful in locating manuscripts and supplying biographical notes. To Miss Evelyn Mitchell I am indebted for assistance in locating poems in periodicals. To Merton College, Oxford, the Armitt Library, Ambleside, and the Fitz Park Trust, Keswick, I am indebted for permission to include poems in their possession.

To Mr. Frederick Page I am particularly indebted for a careful reading and for advice in editorial matters.

To Professor Alfred Senn of the University of Pennsylvania I am grateful for assistance in identifying German poems.

To Mr. C. J. Connelly of the Manuscript Room of the British Museum I am especially indebted for expert assistance in deciphering difficult passages in the manuscripts and for other work of a bibliographical nature.

Finally I wish to pay special tribute to my wife for her co-operation in reading and transcribing manuscripts and in preparing the text for publication.

EARL LESLIE GRIGGS,
University of Pennsylvania.

October, 1941.

CONTENTS

PART I
POEMS PUBLISHED BY HARTLEY COLERIDGE IN 1833

PART II
POSTHUMOUS POEMS PUBLISHED BY DERWENT COLERIDGE IN 1851

PART III

UNPUBLISHED AND UNCOLLECTED POEMS

PART I
POEMS PUBLISHED BY HARTLEY COLERIDGE
IN 1833

I

DEDICATORY SONNET TO S. T. COLERIDGE[1]

FATHER, and Bard revered! to whom I owe,
Whate'er it be, my little art of numbers,
Thou, in thy night-watch o'er my cradled slumbers,[2]
Didst meditate the verse that lives to shew,
(And long shall live, when we alike are low)
Thy prayer how ardent, and thy hope how strong,
That I should learn of Nature's self the song,
The lore which none but Nature's pupils know.

The prayer was heard: I 'wander'd like a breeze',
By mountain brooks and solitary meres,
And gather'd there the shapes and phantasies
Which, mixt with passions of my sadder years,
Compose this book. If good therein there be,
That good, my sire, I dedicate to thee.

[1] Hartley Coleridge used this sonnet in dedicating a volume of poems to his father in 1833; this volume was the only one published during Hartley Coleridge's lifetime.
[2] Alluding to the poem called 'Frost at Midnight', by S. T. Coleridge. The reference is especially to the following lines:

But thou, my babe! shalt wander like a breeze,
By lakes and sandy shores, beneath the crags
Of ancient mountain, and beneath the clouds
Which image in their bulk both lakes, and shores,
And mountain crags: so shalt thou see and hear
The lovely shapes and sounds intelligible
Of that eternal language, which thy God
Utters, who from eternity doth teach
Himself in all, and all things in himself.

As far as regards the *habitats* of my childhood, these lines, written at Nether Stowey, were almost prophetic. But poets are *not* prophets. [Note by Hartley Coleridge.]

II

TO WORDSWORTH[1]

THERE have been poets that in verse display
The elemental forms of human passions:
Poets have been, to whom the fickle fashions
And all the wilful humours of the day
Have furnish'd matter for a polish'd lay:
And many are the smooth elaborate tribe
Who, emulous of thee, the shape describe,
And fain would every shifting hue pourtray
Of restless Nature. But, thou mighty Seer!
'Tis thine to celebrate the thoughts that make
The life of souls, the truths for whose sweet sake
We to ourselves and to our God are dear.
Of Nature's inner shrine thou art the priest,
Where most she works when we perceive her least.[2]

---

[1] Another version of this poem in Hartley Coleridge's handwriting reads:

TO WORDSWORTH

There have been poets, that in verse display
The elemental forms of human passions;
Poets there are, to whom the fleeting fashions
And all the humours of the fickle day
Have furnish'd matter for a polish'd lay;
And many are the smooth elaborate tribe
Who—emulous of thee, the shapes describe
And fain would fire the hues, that mark the way
Which Nature travels. But thou mighty Seer
Ill can they know, thy own peculiar merit—
Who cannot find, in all things that appear
The hidden might of aye-creating spirit;
Thankful am I—to thee, and such as thee,
For more than half the beauty that I see.

[2] Thou worshippest at the Temple's inner shrine,
God being with thee, when we know it not.
—*Wordsworth's Sonnets*. [Note by Hartley Coleridge.]

III

TO SHAKSPEARE

THE soul of man is larger than the sky,
Deeper than ocean, or the abysmal dark
Of the unfathom'd centre. Like that Ark,
Which in its sacred hold uplifted high,
O'er the drown'd hills, the human family,
And stock reserved of every living kind,
So, in the compass of the single mind,
The seeds and pregnant forms in essence lie,
That make all worlds. Great Poet, 'twas thy art
To know thyself, and in thyself to be
Whate'er love, hate, ambition, destiny,
Or the firm, fatal purpose of the heart,
Can make of Man. Yet thou wert still the same,
Serene of thought, unhurt by thy own flame.

IV

LIBERTY

SAY, What is Freedom? What the right of souls
Which all who know are bound to keep, or die,
And who knows not, is dead? In vain ye pry
In musty archives, or retentive scrolls,
Charters and statutes, constitutions, rolls,
And remnants of the old world's history:—
These show what has been, not what ought to be,
Or teach at best how wiser Time controuls
Man's futile purposes. As vain the search
Of restless factions, who, in lawless will,
Fix the foundations of a creedless church—
A lawless rule—an anarchy of ill:
But what is Freedom? Rightly understood,
A universal license to be good.

V

NIGHT

THE crackling embers on the hearth are dead;
The indoor note of industry is still;
The latch is fast; upon the window sill
The small birds wait not for their daily bread;
The voiceless flowers[1]—how quietly they shed
Their nightly odours;—and the household rill
Murmurs continuous dulcet sounds that fill
The vacant expectation, and the dread
Of listening night. And haply now she sleeps;
For all the garrulous noises of the air
Are hush'd in peace; the soft dew silent weeps,
Like hopeless lovers for a maid so fair—
Oh! that I were the happy dream that creeps
To her soft heart, to find my image there.[2]

[1] In the 'Bride's Tragedy,' by Thomas Beddoes, of Pembroke College, Oxon, occurs a hypothetical simile which some prose-witted dunce of a reviewer thought proper to assail with great animosity. Something, I forget what, is
Like flower's voices—*if they could but speak.*
Whoever feels the beauty of that line, has a soul for poetry. [Note by Hartley Coleridge.]

[2] On a copy of this sonnet Hartley Coleridge noted, 'from the German of Ludwig Tieck.' He seems to have been inspired by Tieck's poem, *Schlaflied.* Concerning Tieck, Hartley wrote elsewhere: 'I well remember Tieck. He was at Highgate in 1816. He was then an elderly looking man but perhaps his infirmity increased his apparent age, for he was sorely bent and crippled. As he talked in German and my father in English I could only understand the drift of his more interesting discourses though his English was quite intelligible. Rarely have I seen S.T.C. so well fitted with a companion. Prepossessed in favour of every thing German he found in Tieck an admirer of Kant and Schelling, a believer in Mesmerism, an assertor of Shakespeare's judgment no less than of his genius. I hope however that Tieck's countrymen do not suppose that he derived all his reveries concerning Shakespeare from S.T.C.'

VI

IT must be so,—my infant love must find
In my own breast a cradle and a grave;
Like a rich jewel hid beneath the wave,
Or rebel spirit bound within the rind
Of some old wreathed oak, or fast enshrin'd
In the cold durance of an echoing cave:—
Yea, better thus than cold disdain to brave:—
Or worse,—to taint the quiet of that mind,
That decks its temple with unearthly grace.
Together must we dwell, my dream and I,—
Unknown must live, and unlamented die,
Rather than soil the lustre of that face,
Or drive that laughing dimple from its place,
Or heave that white breast with a painful sigh.

VII

TO A FRIEND[1]

WHEN we were idlers with the loitering rills,
The need of human love we little noted:
Our love was nature; and the peace that floated
On the white mist, and dwelt upon the hills,[2]
To sweet accord subdued our wayward wills:
One soul was ours, one mind, one heart devoted,
That, wisely doating, ask'd not why it doated,
And ours the unknown joy, which knowing kills.
But now I find, how dear thou wert to me;
That man is more than half of nature's treasure,
Of that fair Beauty which no eye can see,
Of that sweet music which no ear can measure;
And now the streams may sing for others' pleasure,
The hills sleep on in their eternity.

[1] This sonnet . . . [was] addressed to R. S. Jameson, Esq., on occasion of meeting him in London after a separation of some years. He was the favourite companion of my boyhood, the active friend and sincere counsellor of my youth. 'Though seas between us broad ha' roll'd' since we 'travell'd side by side' last, I trust the sight of this little volume will give rise to recollections that will make him ten years younger. He is now Judge Advocate at Dominica, and husband of Mrs. Jameson, authoress of the *Diary of an Ennuyée, Loves of the Poets,* and other agreeable productions. [Note by Hartley Coleridge.]

[2]   Love had he found in huts, where poor men lie,
    His daily teachers had been woods and rills,
    The silence that is in the starry sky,
    The peace that sleeps upon the dewy hills.
—*Wordsworth's Song at the Feast of Brougham Castle.* [Note by Hartley Coleridge.]

VIII

How long I sail'd, and never took a thought
To what port I was bound! Secure as sleep,
I dwelt upon the bosom of the deep
And perilous sea. And though my ship was fraught
With rare and precious fancies, jewels brought
From fairy-land, no course I cared to keep,
Nor changeful wind nor tide I heeded ought,
But joy'd to feel the merry billows leap,
And watch the sun-beams dallying with the waves;
Or haply dream what realms beneath may lie
Where the clear ocean is an emerald sky,
And mermaids warble in their coral caves,
Yet vainly woo to me their secret home;—
And sweet it were for ever so to roam.

IX

FROM COUNTRY TO TOWN
Written in Leeds, July, 1932.[1]

I LEFT the land where men with Nature dwelling,
Know not how much they love her lovely forms—
Nor heed the history of forgotten storms,
On the blank folds inscribed of drear Helvellyn;
I sought the town, where toiling, buying, selling—
Getting and spending, poising hope and fear,
Make but one season of the live-long year.
Now for the brook from moss-girt fountain welling,
I see the foul stream hot with sleepless trade;
For the slow creeping vapours of the morn,
Black hurrying smoke, in opake mass up-borne,
O'er dinning engines hangs, a stifling shade—
Yet Nature lives e'en here, and will not part
From her best home, the lowly-loving heart.

[1] Except for a few months' residence in Leeds, Hartley Coleridge never left the Lake Country after he had been 'exiled' there in 1823. While at Leeds he prepared his poems for the Press and wrote and published *Biographia Borealis*, but he was unhappy and welcomed his return to Grasmere.

X

FROM COUNTRY TO TOWN
(CONTINUED)

'Tis strange to me, who long have seen no face,
That was not like a book, whose every page
I knew by heart, a kindly common-place,
And faithful record of progressive age—
To wander forth, and view an unknown race;
Of all that I have been, to find no trace,
No footstep of my by-gone pilgrimage.
Thousands I pass, and no one stays his pace
To tell me that the day is fair, or rainy;
Each one his object seeks with anxious chase,
And I have not a common hope with any:
Thus like one drop of oil upon a flood,
In uncommunicating solitude,
Single am I amid the countless many.

XI

Long time a child, and still a child, when years
Had painted manhood on my cheek, was I,—
For yet I lived like one not born to die;
A thriftless prodigal of smiles and tears,
No hope I needed, and I knew no fears.
But sleep, though sweet, is only sleep, and waking,
I waked to sleep no more, at once o'ertaking
The vanguard of my age, with all arrears
Of duty on my back. Nor child, nor man,
Nor youth, nor sage, I find my head is grey,
For I have lost the race I never ran:
A rathe December blights my lagging May;
And still I am a child, tho' I be old,
Time is my debtor for my years untold.

XII

SONNET BY A YOUNG OLD MAN

YOUTH, thou art fled,—but where are all the charms
Which, tho' with thee they came, and pass'd with thee,
Should leave a perfume and sweet memory
Of what they have been?—All thy boons and harms
Have perish'd quite.—Thy oft renew'd alarms
Forsake the fluttering echo.—Smiles and tears
Die on my cheek, or, petrified with years,
Shew the dull woe which no compassion warms,
The mirth none shares. Yet could a wish, a thought,
Unravel all the complex web of age,—
Could all the characters that Time hath wrought
Be clean effaced from my memorial page
By one short word, the word I would not say,
I thank my God, because my hairs are grey.

Rydal Mount, New Year's day, 1829.

XIII

I thank my God because my hairs are grey!
But have grey hairs brought wisdom? Doth the flight
Of summer birds, departed while the light
Of life is lingering on the middle way,
Predict the harvest nearer by a day?
Will the rank weeds of hopeless appetite
Droop at the glance and venom of the blight
That made the vermeil bloom, the flush so gay,
Dim and unlovely as a dead worm's shroud?
Or is my heart, that, wanting hope, has lost
The strength and rudder of resolve, at peace?
Is it no longer wrathful, vain, and proud?
Is it a Sabbath, or untimely frost,
That makes the labour of the soul to cease?

XIV

———

WHY should I murmur at my lot forlorn?
The self-same Fate that doom'd me to be poor
Endues me with a spirit to endure
All, and much more, than is or has been borne
By better men, of want, or worldly scorn.
My soul has faith, my body has the nerve
To brave the penance that my sins deserve.
And yet my helpless state I deeply mourn:
Well could I bear to be deserted quite,—
Less should I blame my fortune were it worse;—
But taking all, it yet hath left me friends,
For whom I needs must mourn the wayward spite
That hides my purpose in an empty purse,
Since what I grateful wish, in wishing ends.

XV

MAY, 1832

———

Is this the merry May of tale and song?
Chill breathes the North—the sky looks chilly blue,
The waters wear a cold and iron hue,
Or wrinkle as the crisp wave creeps along,
Much like an ague fit. The starry throng
Of flow'rets droop o'erdone with drenching dew,
Or close their leaves at noon, as if they knew,
And felt in helpless wrath, the season's wrong.
Yet in the half-clad woods the busy birds
Chirping with all their might to keep them warm;
The young hare flitting from her ferny form;
The vernal lowing of the amorous herds;
And swelling buds impatient of delay,
Declare it should be, tho' it is not, May.

XVI

NOVEMBER

THE mellow year is hasting to its close;
The little birds have almost sung their last,
Their small notes twitter in the dreary blast—
That shrill-piped harbinger of early snows;
The patient beauty of the scentless rose,[1]
Oft with the Morn's hoar crystal quaintly glass'd,
Hangs, a pale mourner for the summer past,
And makes a little summer where it grows:
In the chill sunbeam of the faint brief day
The dusky waters shudder as they shine,
The russet leaves obstruct the straggling way
Of oozy brooks, which no deep banks define,
And the gaunt woods, in ragged, scant array,
Wrap their old limbs with sombre ivy twine.

---

[1] The Chinese, or monthly rose, so frequently seen clustering round the cottage-porch, both in the remotest vales and in the immediate outskirts of busy, smoky towns, is almost destitute of scent. The manner in which this cheerful foreigner perseveres in the habits of a warmer climate, through all vicissitudes of ours, is a remarkable instance of vegetable nationality. [Note by Hartley Coleridge.]

XVII

THE FIRST BIRTH DAY

THE Sun, sweet girl, hath run his year-long race
Through the vast nothing of the eternal sky—
Since the glad hearing of the first faint cry
Announc'd a stranger from the unknown place
Of unborn souls. How blank was then the face,
How uninform'd the weak light-shunning eye,
That wept and saw not. Poor mortality
Begins to mourn before it knows its case,
Prophetic in its ignorance.[1] But soon
The hospitalities of earth[2] engage
The banish'd spirit in its new exile—
Pass some few changes of the fickle Moon,
The merry babe has learn'd its Mother's smile,
Its Father's frown, its Nurse's mimic rage.

[1]   Thou know'st, the first time that we smell the air
   We waule and cry.
   When we are born, we cry that we are come
   To this great stage of fools.
                        Shakespeare: *King Lear*, Act IV.

The thought, which is obvious enough indeed, occurs in an older writer than Shakspeare, and might probably be traced to some of the fathers, or to Seneca. Robert Greene reproaches Shakspeare with reading Seneca *done* into English. [Note by Hartley Coleridge.]

[2]   Earth fills her lap with pleasures of her own.
   Yearnings she hath in her own natural kind,
   And even with something of a mother's mind,
       And no unworthy aim,
       The homely nurse doth all she can
   To make her foster-child, her inmate man,
   Forget the glories he hath known,
   And that imperial palace whence he came.
                   —Wordsworth. [Note by Hartley Coleridge.]

XVIII

TO A LOFTY BEAUTY, FROM HER POOR KINSMAN[1]

FAIR maid, had I not heard thy baby cries,
Nor seen thy girlish, sweet vicissitude,
Thy mazy motions, striving to elude,
Yet wooing still a parent's watchful eyes,
Thy humours, many as the opal's dyes,
And lovely all;—methinks thy scornful mood,
And bearing high of stately womanhood,—
Thy brow, where Beauty sits to tyrannize
O'er humble love, had made me sadly fear thee;
For never sure was seen a royal bride,
Whose gentleness gave grace to so much pride—
My very thoughts would tremble to be near thee:
But when I see thee at thy father's side,
Old times unqueen thee, and old loves endear thee.

[1] This sonnet is addressed to Edith Southey.

XIX

REPLY[1]

Ah! well it is, since she is gone,
    She can return no more,
To see the face so dim and wan,
    That was so warm before.

Familiar things would all seem strange,
    And pleasure past be woe;
A record sad of ceaseless change,
    Is all the world below.

The very hills, they are not now
    The hills which once they were;
They change as we are changed, or how
    Could we the burden bear?

Ye deem the dead are ashy pale,
    Cold denizens of gloom—
But what are ye, who live to wail,
    And weep upon their tomb?

She pass'd away, like morning dew,
    Before the sun was high;
So brief her time, she scarcely knew
    The meaning of a sigh.

As round the rose its soft perfume,
    Sweet love around her floated;
Admired she grew—while mortal doom
    Crept on, unfear'd, unnoted.

Love was her guardian Angel here,
    But love to death resign'd her;
Tho' love was kind, why should we fear,
    But holy death is kinder?

[1] This poem was originally connected with another one on the death of Isabel Southey, and the two poems were entitled 'Question' and 'Reply'.

XX

AN OLD MAN'S WISH

I HAVE lived, and I have loved,
    Have lived and loved in vain;
Some joys, and many woes have proved,
    That may not be again;
My heart is cold, my eye is sere,
Joy wins no smile, and grief no tear.

Fain would I hope, if hope I could,
    If sure to be deceived,
There's comfort in a thought of good,
    Tho' 'tis not quite believed;
For sweet is hope's wild warbled air,
But, oh! its echo is despair.

XXI

SONG

SHE is not fair to outward view
    As many maidens be,
Her loveliness I never knew
    Until she smil'd on me;
Oh! then I saw her eye was bright,
A well of love, a spring of light.

But now her looks are coy and cold,
    To mine they ne'er reply,
And yet I cease not to behold
    The love-light in her eye:
Her very frowns are fairer far,
Than smiles of other maidens are.

XXII

STANZAS

SHE was a queen of noble Nature's crowning,
A smile of her's was like an act of grace;
She had no winsome looks, no pretty frowning,
Like daily beauties of the vulgar race:
But if she smiled, a light was on her face,
A clear, cool kindliness, a lunar beam
Of peaceful radiance, silvering o'er the stream
Of human thought with unabiding glory;
Not quite a waking truth, not quite a dream,
A visitation, bright and transitory.

But she is changed,—hath felt the touch of sorrow,
No love hath she, no understanding friend;
Oh grief! when heaven is forced of earth to borrow
What the poor niggard earth has not to lend;
But when the stalk is snapt, the rose must bend.
The tallest flower that skyward rears its head,
Grows from the common ground, and there must shed
Its delicate petals. Cruel fate, too surely,
That they should find so base a bridal bed,
Who lived in virgin pride, so sweet and purely.

She had a brother, and a tender father,
And she was lov'd, but not as others are
From whom we ask return of love,—but rather
As one might love a dream; a phantom-fair
Of something exquisitely strange and rare,
Which all were glad to look on, men and maids,
Yet no one claim'd—as oft, in dewy glades
The peering primrose, like a sudden gladness,
Gleams on the soul—yet unregarded fades—[1]
The joy is ours, but all its own the sadness.

'Tis vain to say—her worst of grief is only
The common lot, which all the world have known;
To her 'tis more, because her heart is lonely,
And yet she hath no strength to stand alone,—
Once she had playmates, fancies of her own,
And she did love them. They are past away
As Fairies vanish at the break of day;
And like a spectre of an age departed,
Or unsphered Angel woefully astray—
She glides along—the solitary hearted.

[1] 'And the rathe primrose that forsaken dies.'—*Lycidas.* [Note by Hartley
Coleridge.]

XXIII

SONG[1]

'TIS sweet to hear the merry lark,
   That bids a blithe good-morrow;
But sweeter to hark, in the twinkling dark,
   To the soothing song of sorrow.
Oh nightingale! What doth she ail?
   And is she sad or jolly?
For ne'er on earth was sound of mirth
   So like to melancholy.

The merry lark, he soars on high,
   No worldly thought o'ertakes him;
He sings aloud to the clear blue sky,
   And the daylight that awakes him.
As sweet a lay, as loud, as gay,
   The nightingale is trilling;
With feeling bliss, no less than his,
   Her little heart is thrilling.

Yet ever and anon, a sigh,
   Peers through her lavish mirth;
For the lark's bold song is of the sky,
   And hers is of the earth.
By night and day, she tunes her lay,
   To drive away all sorrow;
For bliss, alas! to-night must pass,
   And woe may come to-morrow.

[1] Among the controversies of the day, not the least important is that respecting the song of the Nightingale. It is debated whether the notes of this bird are of a joyous or a melancholy expression. He who has spoken so decisively of 'the merry Nightingale', must forgive my somewhat unfilial inclination towards the elder and more common opinion. No doubt the sensations of the bird while singing are pleasurable, but the question is, What is the feeling which its song, considered as a succession of sounds produced by an instrument, is calculated to carry to a human listener? When we speak of a pathetic strain of music, we do not mean that either the fiddler or his fiddle are unhappy, but that the tones or intervals of the air are such as the mind associates with tearful sympathies. At the same time, I utterly deny that the voice of philomel expresses present pain. I could never have imagined that the pretty creature 'sets her breast against a thorn', and could not have perpetrated the diabolical story of Tereus. In fact, nature is very little obliged to the heathen mythology. The constant *anthropomorphism* of the Greek religion sorely perplexed the ancient conceptions of natural beauty. A river is turned into a god, who is still too much of a river to be quite a god. It is a statue of ice in a continual state of liquefaction. [Note by Hartley Coleridge.]

XXIV
NEW-YEAR'S DAY

WHILE the bald trees stretch forth their long, lank
    arms,
And starving birds peck nigh the reeky farms:
While houseless cattle paw the yellow field,
Or coughing shiver in the pervious bield,
And nought more gladsome in the hedge is seen,
Than the dark holly's grimly glistening green—
At such a time, the ancient year goes by
To join its parents in eternity—
At such a time the merry year is born,
Like the bright berry from the naked thorn.

The bells ring out; the hoary steeple rocks—
Hark! the long story of a score of clocks;
For, once a year, the village clocks agree,
E'en clocks unite to sound the hour of glee—
And every cottage has a light awake:
Unusual stars long flicker o'er the lake;
The moon on high, if any moon be there,
May peep, or wink—no mortal now will care—
For 'tis the season, when the nights are long;
There's time, ere morn, for each to sing his song.

The year departs, a blessing on its head,
We mourn not for it, for it is not dead:
Dead? What is that? A word to joy unknown,
Which love abhors, and faith will never own.
A word, whose meaning sense could never find,
That has no truth in matter, nor in mind.
The passing breezes gone as soon as felt,
The flakes of snow that in the soft air melt,
The wave that whitening curls its frothy crest,
And falls to sleep upon its mother's breast.
The smile that sinks into a maiden's eye,
They come, they go, they change, they do not die.
So the Old Year—that fond and formal name,
Is with us yet, another and the same.

And are the thoughts, that ever more are fleeing,
The moments that make up our being's being,
The silent workings of unconscious love,
Or the dull hate which clings and will not move,
In the dark caverns of the gloomy heart,
The fancies wild and horrible, which start
Like loathsome reptiles from their crankling holes,
From foul, neglected corners of our souls,
Are these less vital than the wave or wind,
Or snow that melts and leaves no trace behind?
Oh! let them perish all, or pass away,
And let our spirits feel a New-Year's day.

A New-Year's day—'tis but a term of art,
An arbitrary line upon the chart
Of Time's unbounded sea—fond fancy's creature,
To reason alien, and unknown to nature.
Nay—'tis a joyful day, a day of hope!
Bound, merry dancer, like an Antelope;
And as that lovely creature, far from man,
Gleams through the spicy groves of Hindostan,
Flash through the labyrinth of the mazy dance,
With foot as nimble, and as keen a glance.

And we, whom many New-Year's days have told
The sober truth, that we are growing old—
For this one night—aye—and for many more,
Will be as jocund as we were of yore:
Kind hearts can make December blithe as May,
And in each morrow find a New-Year's day.

XXV
WRITTEN ON THE FIRST OF NOVEMBER,
1820

HAIL, dark November! spurious progeny
Of Phœbus and old Night,—thou sable mourner,
That lead'st the funeral pageant of the year,—
Thou Winter's herald, sent before thy lord
To bid the earth prepare for his dread presence,—
I gladly wish thee welcome, for thou wear'st
No flaunting smile to mock pale Melancholy,
Which ever loves its likeness, and derives
From most discomfort, truest consolation.

The world is heartsick, and o'erwearied Nature
Bears, in her lost abandonment, the mark
Of ills expected, and of pleasures past,
And, like a late-repenting prodigal,
Deals out with thrift enforc'd the scant remains
Of lavish'd wealth, sighing to think upon
The riotous days, that left no joy unrifled,
No store reserv'd, to comfort poor old age:
The tip-toe levity of Spring, flower-deck'd,
And Summer's pride, and Autumn's hospitality
Have eat up all.

            And now her festal robes
Are worn to rags,—poor rents of tatter'd state,
Telling a tale of mad, luxurious waste,
Yet not enough to cover nakedness,—
A garb of many hues, and wretched all.
There is a desperate patience in her look,
And straggling smiles, or rather ghosts of smiles,
Display the sadness of her wrinkled visage.
Anon, with gusty rage, she casts away
Her motley weeds, and tears her thin grey locks,
And treads her squalid splendour in the mire;
Then weeps amain to think what she has done,
Doom'd to cold penance in a sheet of snow.

XXVI

DEATH-BED REFLECTIONS OF MICHEL-ANGELO

Not that my hand could make of stubborn stone
Whate'er of Gods the shaping thought conceives;
Not that my skill by pictured lines hath shown
All terrors that the guilty soul believes;
Not that my art, by blended light and shade,
Express'd the world as it was newly made;
Not that my verse profoundest truth could teach,
In the soft accents of the lover's speech;
Not that I rear'd a temple for mankind,
To meet and pray in, borne by every wind—
Affords me peace—I count my gain but loss,
For that vast love, that hangs upon the Cross.

PART II
POSTHUMOUS POEMS PUBLISHED BY DERWENT COLERIDGE IN 1851

I

COLERIDGE THE POET[1]

I<small>F</small> when thou wert a living man, my sire,
I shrank unequal from the task to praise
The ripening worth of thy successive days,
What shall I do since that imputed fire,
Extinct its earthly aliment, doth aspire,
Purged from the passionate subject of all lays,
From all that fancy fashions and obeys,
Beyond the argument of mortal lyre?
If while a militant and suffering saint,
Thou walk'dst the earth in penury and pain,
Thy great Idea was too high a strain
For my infirmity, how shall I dare
Thy perfect and immortal self to paint?
Less awful task to 'draw empyreal air'.

October 28, [1836.]

II

WRITTEN ON THE ANNIVERSARY OF OUR FATHER'S DEATH

S<small>TILL</small> for the world he lives, and lives in bliss,
For God and for himself. Ten years and three
Have now elapsed since he was dead to me
And all that were on earth intensely his.
Not in the dim domain of Gloomy Dis,
The death-god of the ever-guessing Greek,
Nor in the paradise of Houris sleek
I think of him whom I most sorely miss.
The sage, the poet, lives for all mankind,
As long as truth is true, or beauty fair.
The soul that ever sought its God to find
Has found Him now—no matter how, or where.
Yet can I not but mourn because he died
That was my father, should have been my guide.

1847

[1] Hartley Coleridge intended this sonnet as an introduction to his proposed essay on Coleridge to be prefixed to the second edition of the *Biographia Literaria.* While the essay was never completed fragments of it remain. They are published in an article, 'Hartley Coleridge on His Father'. Cf. *Publications of the Modern Language Association*, Vol. XLVI, No. 4 (December, 1931).

III

OH! my dear mother, art thou still awake?
Or art thou sleeping on thy Maker's arm,—
Waiting in slumber for the shrill alarm
Ordain'd to give the world its final shake?
Art thou with 'interlunar night' opaque
Clad like a worm while waiting for its wings;
Or doth the shadow of departed things
Dwell on thy soul as on a breezeless lake!
Oh! would that I could see thee in thy heaven
For one brief hour, and know I was forgiven
For all the pain and doubt and rankling shame
Which I have caused to make thee weep or sigh.
Bootless the wish! for where thou art on high,
Sin casts no shadow, sorrow hath no name.

September, 1846 [*composed presumably on the first
anniversary of his mother's death.*]

IV

ON MY TWIN NIECE AND NEPHEW, DYING WITHIN AN HOUR AFTER BIRTH[1]

BUT born to die, they hardly breath'd the air,
Till God revoked the mandate of their doom.
A brief imprisonment within the womb
Of human life was all their destined share.
Two whiter souls unstain'd with sin or care
Shall never blossom from the fertile tomb;—
Sweet buds that not on earth were meant to bloom,
So swiftly Heaven recall'd the spotless pair.
Let man that on his own desert relies,
And deems himself the creditor of God,
Think how these babes have earn'd their paradise,
How small the work of their small period:
Their very cradle was the hopeful grave,
God only made them for His Christ to save.

[1] This sonnet was a part of a metrical letter to his sister Sara Coleridge, and refers to the death of her twins, Florence and Berkeley. See *Letters of Hartley Coleridge*, p. 170.

V

TO WILLIAM WORDSWORTH

YES, mighty Poet, we have read thy lines,
And felt our hearts the better for the reading.
A friendly spirit, from thy soul proceeding,
Unites our souls; the light from thee that shines
Like the first break of morn, dissolves, combines
All creatures with a living flood of beauty.
For thou hast proved that purest joy is duty,
And love a fondling, that the trunk entwines
Of sternest fortitude. Oh, what must be
Thy glory here, and what the huge reward
In that blest region of thy poesy?
For long as man exists, immortal Bard,
Friends, husbands, wives, in sadness or in glee,
Shall love each other more for loving thee.

March 26, 1839.

VI

RYDAL

NIGH to the mansion of a titled dame,
A charitable lady, though recluse,
Begirt with trees too reverend for use,
A village lies, and Rydal is its name.
Its natives know not what is meant by fame;
They little know how men in future time
Will venerate the spot, where prose and rhyme
Too strong for aught but Heaven itself to tame,
Gush'd from a mighty Poet. Yet all calm,
Calm as the antique trunks whose hollow age
The woodman spares, sweet thoughts on every page
Breathe for the soul admonitory balm.
'Tis Nature teaching what she never knew;
The beautiful is good, the good is true.

VII

HOMER

FAR from the sight of earth, yet bright and plain
As the clear noon-day sun, an 'orb of song'
Lovely and bright is seen amid the throng
Of lesser stars, that rise, and wax, and wane,
The transient rulers of the fickle main;—
One constant light gleams through the dark and long
And narrow aisle of memory. How strong,
How fortified with all the numerous train
Of truths wert thou, Great Poet of mankind,
Who told'st in verse as mighty as the sea,
And various as the voices of the wind,
The strength of passion rising in the glee
Of battle. Fear was glorified by thee,
And Death is lovely in thy tale enshrined.

VIII

THINK upon Death, 'tis good to think of Death,
But better far to think upon the Dead.
Death is a spectre with a bony head,
Or the mere mortal body without breath,
The state foredoom'd of every son of Seth,
Decomposition—dust, or dreamless sleep.
But the dear Dead are they for whom we weep,
For whom I credit all the Bible saith.
Dead is my father, dead is my good mother,
And what on earth have I to do but die?
But if by grace I reach the blessed sky,
I fain would see the same, and not another;
The very father that I used to see,
The mother that has nursed me on her knee.

IX

A LONELY wanderer upon earth am I,
The waif of nature—like uprooted weed
Borne by the stream, or like a shaken reed,
A frail dependent of the fickle sky.
Far, far away, are all my natural kin:
The mother that erewhile hath hush'd my cry,
Almost hath grown a mere fond memory.
Where is my sister's smile? my brother's boisterous din?
Ah! nowhere now. A matron grave and sage,
A holy mother is that sister sweet.
And that bold brother is a pastor meet
To guide, instruct, reprove a sinful age,
Almost I fear what yet I fain would greet;
So far astray hath been my pilgrimage.

X

LET me not deem that I was made in vain,
Or that my Being was an accident,
Which Fate, in working its sublime intent,
Not wish'd to be, to hinder would not deign.
Each drop uncounted in a storm of rain
Hath its own mission, and is duly sent
To its own leaf or blade, not idly spent
'Mid myriad dimples on the shipless main.
The very shadow of an insect's wing,
For which the violet cared not while it stay'd,
Yet felt the lighter for its vanishing,
Proved that the sun was shining by its shade:
Then can a drop of the eternal spring,
Shadow of living lights, in vain be made?

XI

———

WHEN I review the course that I have run,
And count the loss of all my wasted days,
I find no argument for joy or praise
In whatsoe'er my soul hath thought or done.
I am a desert, and the kindly sun
On me hath vainly spent his fertile rays.
Then wherefore do I tune my idle lays,
Or dream that haply I may be the one
Of the vain thousands, that shall win a place
Among the Poets,—that a single rhyme
Of my poor wit's devising may find grace
To breed high memories in the womb of time?
But to confound the time the Muse I woo;
Then 'tis but just that time confound me too.

XII

MUSIC

SWEET music steals along the yielding soul,
Like the brisk wind that sows autumnal seeds;
And it hath tones like vernal rain that feeds
The light green vale, ordain'd ere long to roll
In golden waves o'er many a wealthy rood;
And tones it hath, that make a lonely hour
The silent dwelling of some lovely flower,
Sweet Hermitess of Forest solitude.
I loved sweet Music when I was a child,
For then my mother used to sing to me:
I loved it better when a youth so wild,
With thoughts of love it did so well agree;
Fain would I love it to my latest day,
If it would teach me to believe and pray.

XIII

Hast thou not seen an aged rifted tower,
Meet habitation for the Ghost of Time,
Where fearful ravage makes decay sublime,
And destitution wears the face of power?
Yet is the fabric deck'd with many a flower
Of fragrance wild, and many-dappled hue,
Gold streak'd with iron-brown, and nodding blue,
Making each ruinous chink a fairy bower.
E'en such a thing methinks I fain would be,
Should Heaven appoint me to a lengthen'd age;
So old in look, that Young and Old may see
The record of my closing pilgrimage:
Yet, to the last, a rugged wrinkled thing
To which young sweetness may delight to cling!

XIV

Ah me! It is the saddest thing on earth
To see a change where much is yet unchanged,
To mark a face, not alter'd, but estranged
From its own wonted self, by its own hearth
So sadly smiling, like the ghost of mirth,
That cannot quite desert its long abode.
The very sigh that lifts the weary load
Of pain, and loosens the constraining girth
Within the breast, a semi-tone of laughter;
Though joy to woe, as light to shade is turn'd
The trick of joy is not so soon unlearn'd:
The substance flits, the shadow lingers after.
The soul once rich in joy, though poor it be,
Will yet be bounteous in its poverty.

XV

WRITTEN IN A SEASON OF PUBLIC DISTURBANCE

CALM is the sky: the trees are very calm.
The mountains seem as they would melt away,
So soft their outline mingles with the day.
Surely no sound less holy than a psalm
Should interrupt the stillness and the balm
Of such a morn, whose grave monastic grey
Clothes the meek east in garment meet to pray
With sweet humility, without a qualm.
And yet, even now, in this most blessed hour,
Who knows but that the murderous shot is sped
In the fell jar of poverty and power?
The man but now that lived, may now be dead.
Has Nature of her human brood no care,
That on their bloody deeds she smiles so fair?

August 19, 1842.

XVI

TO MRS. CHARLES FOX[1]

Now the old trees are striving to be young,
And the gay mosses of the Christmas days
To the fresh primrose must forego their praise:
Now every flower by vernal poets sung,
And every bird the pushing woods among,
And all the many-dappled banks and braes,
Recall remembrance of immortal lays,
But speak to me in a forgotten tongue.
Yea, dearest lady, they do speak to me
As to a banish'd man that hath forgot
Almost his mother's language, and cannot,
Without sore pain and stress of memory,
Reply to words that yet he hears with joy,
And by their strangeness make him half a boy.

---

[1] This sonnet was enclosed in a letter from Ambleside, dated April 9, 1842, and reading in part: 'The mountains stand where they did and I suppose that the lights and shadows repeat themselves after their old fashion but they are not the same mountains to me as they were when you had your little boat on Grasmere Lake—and could laugh at my awkwardness in handling the oars. They are grown old like myself. When a boy I thought a mountain was nothing but to be climbed—Snow was to make snowballs of—Ice for me to slide on. In riper youth I thought of them as Powers in all their beauty and all their ruggedness witnessing and authorizing a kindred power in myself An imagination, that as it enabled me to make one beauty of all the uncountable beauties great and small—that were asserting themselves around me, combining the Celandine at my feet, with the shelving crag above me, might enable me not to create—for that is a word not applicable to any effluence of the human mind—but to generate a correspondent world—in which the images derived from outer things should be not causes but emblems of the things within—and Love itself—a sacrament of that love divine which merges itself in its object. Now the mountains are to me but mighty monuments of what has been—and what might have been and might be yet had I living objects I love near enough—but no matter.'

XVII
THE VERNAL SHOWER

WELCOME once more, my pretty Lady Spring:
So young a Spring we have not seen for years.
Even thy brief morning fit of girlish tears
Was bright and sweet as droppings from the wing
Of kindly sylph, through ether voyaging
On some good errand to the distant spheres;
And every bud and blade, to which adheres
The pure aspersion, seems a conscious thing,
Renew'd in spirit. Light the birdie leaps,
Shaking translucent gems from every spray;
And merrily down the many-shadow'd steeps
The streamlets whiten, all in new array.
Joy to the vale if Summer do but keep
The bounteous promise of this April day.

Grasmere, April, **1842.**

XVIII
MAY, 1840

A LOVELY morn, so still, so very still,
It hardly seems a growing day of Spring,
Though all the odorous buds are blossoming,
And the small matin birds were glad and shrill
Some hours ago; but now the woodland rill
Murmurs along, the only vocal thing,
Save when the wee wren flits with stealthy wing,
And cons by fits and bits her evening trill.
Lovers might sit on such a morn as this
An hour together, looking at the sky,
Nor dare to break the silence with a kiss,
Long listening for the signal of a sigh;
And the sweet Nun, diffused in voiceless prayer,
Feel her own soul through all the brooding air.

Gill Head.

XIX

How strange the cold ungenial atmosphere,
Beneath the cover of so bright a sky!
Each woodland flower hath oped its little eye;
The very coyest buds of all the year
Have ventured forth to see if all be clear.
Full-leaved the pendant birches droop and sigh;
The oak is clad in vernal majesty;
White-chaliced lilies float upon the mere.
The very warmth that made this world of beauty
Is summon'd to another track of duty,
And leaves a substitute so stern and cold,
We half regret old Winter's honest rule,
The roaring chimney and the log of yule:
May hath such airs as May had not of old.

May 23, 1841.

XX

SEPTEMBER

THE dark green Summer, with its massive hues,
Fades into Autumn's tincture manifold.
A gorgeous garniture of fire and gold
The high slope of the ferny hill indues.
The mists of morn in slumbering layers diffuse
O'er glimmering rock, smooth lake, and spiked array
Of hedge-row thorns, a unity of grey.
All things appear their tangible form to lose
In ghostly vastness. But anon the gloom
Melts, as the Sun puts off his muddy veil;
And now the birds their twittering songs resume,
All Summer silent in the leafy dale.
In Spring they piped of love on every tree,
But now they sing the song of memory.

XXI

ON A CALM DAY TOWARDS THE CLOSE OF THE YEAR

THERE never was an hour of purer peace!
Methinks old Time, in mere mortality,
Gives up the ghost, contented not to be,
And all the pulses of great Nature cease.
Whatever tokens hope, life, or increase,
The gladsome expectation, or the dread
Of chance and change upon to-morrow fed,
Await the expiration of their lease
In dumb, dull apathy. Not on the tree
Stirs the brown leaf; or, if detach'd, it drop,
So very slow it wavers to the ground
One might suppose that central gravity,
Prime law of motion, were about to stop:
Ne'er died a year with spirit so profound.[1]

December 22, 1835.

XXII

CHRISTMAS DAY

WAS it a fancy, bred of vagrant guess,
Or well-remember'd fact, that *He* was born
When half the world was wintry and forlorn,
In Nature's utmost season of distress?
And did the sinful earth indeed confess
Its destitution and its craving need,
Wearing the white and penitential weed,
Meet symbol of judicial barrenness?
So be it; for in truth 'tis ever so,
That when the winter of the soul is bare,
The seed of heaven at first begins to grow,
Peeping abroad in desert of despair.
Full many a flow'ret, good, and sweet, and fair,
Is kindly wrapp'd in coverlet of snow.

[1] Collated with an original manuscript in the possession of the trustees of the Rev. J. H. Clay.

XXIII

DECEMBER 12, 1838

THE poor old year upon its deathbed lies;
Old trees lift up their branches manifold,
Spiry and stern, inveterately old;
Their bare and patient poverty defies
The fickle humour of inconstant skies.
All chill and distant, the great monarch Sun
Beholds the last days of his minion.
What is 't to him how soon the old year dies?
Yet some things are, but lowly things and small,
That wait upon the old year to the last;
Some wee birds pipe a feeble madrigal,
Trilling kind memories of the summer past;
Some duteous flowers put on their best array
To do meet honour to their Lord's decay.

XXIV

TO A SNOW-DROP

YES—punctual to thy time, thou'rt here again
As still thou art, though frost or rain may vary,
Most indefatigable Missionary!
Nor cold can check, nor fog thy pureness stain;
If sluggish snow lie heavy on the plain,
And Icicles blockade the rock-birds aery,
Yet thou, sweet child of hoary January,
Art here to harbinger the laggard train
Of vernal flowers. Beneath the penthouse low
The dripping eaves, and on the sunny slope
Of cottage garden, whether mark'd or no,
Thy meek head bends in undistinguished row.
A Blessing on thee, gentle bud of Hope,
That tells of life, beneath the dead white snow.
                              [*Ambleside*, 1841.]

XXV

THE CELANDINE AND THE DAISY

I LOVE the flowers that Nature gives away
With such a careless bounty: some would deem
She thought them baubles, things of no esteem,
Mere idle followers of unthrifty May.
See in the lane, where geese and donkeys stray,
That golden flower, the countless Celandine:
Though long o'erlook'd, it needs no praise of mine,
For 'tis one mightier poet's joy and theme.
See how the Daisies whiten all yon lea!
A thing so dear to poet and to child,
That when we see it on neglected wild,
We praise old Nature's generosity,
The Celandine one mighty bard may prize;
The Daisy no bard can monopolise.

May, 1846.

XXVI

THE CUCKOO

THOU indefatigable cuckoo! still
Thy iteration says the self-same thing,
And thou art still an utterance of the spring
As constant as a self-determined will.
The quiet patience of a murmuring rill
Had no beginning and will have no ending;
But thou art aye beginning, never blending
With thrush on perch, or lark upon the wing.
Methinks thou art a type of some recluse
Whose notes of adoration never vary:
Who of the gift of speech will make no use
But ever to repeat her Ave Mary.—
Two syllables alone to thee were given,
What mean they in the dialect of heaven?

May 22nd, 1848.

XXVII

TO AN INFANT[1]

SURE 'tis a holy and a healing thought
That fills my heart and mind at sight of thee,
Thou purest abstract of humanity.
Sweet infant, we might deem thy smile was brought
From some far distant Paradise, where nought
Forbad to hope whate'er of good may be,
Where thou could'st know, and feel, and taste, and see
That innocence, which lost, is vainly sought
In this poor world. Yet, if thou wert so good
As love conceives thee, thou hadst ne'er been born;
For sure the Lord of Justice never would
Have doom'd a loyal spirit to be shorn
Of its immortal glories—never could
Exile perfection to an earth forlorn.

XXVIII

TO AN INFANT

WISE is the way of Nature, first to make
This tiny model of what is to be,
A thing that we may love as soon as see,
That seems as passive as a summer lake
When there is not a sigh of wind to shake
The aspen leaf upon the tall slim tree.
Yet who can tell, sweet infant mystery,
What thoughts in thee e'en now begin to wake?
Something already dost thou know of pain,
And, sinless, bear'st the penalty of sin;
And yet as quickly wilt thou smile again
After thy cries, as vanishes the stain
Of breath from steel. So may the peace within
In thy ripe season re-assert its reign.

Sunday, September 3, 1848.

[1] This poem was addressed Mary Ann Green and was written at Ambleside in 1830.

XXIX

THE GOD-CHILD[1]

I stood beside thee in the holy place,
And saw the holy sprinkling on thy brow,
And was both bond and witness to the vow
Which own'd thy need, confirm'd thy claim of grace;
That sacred sign which time shall not efface
Declared thee His, to whom all angels bow,
Who bade the herald saint the rite allow
To the sole sinless of all Adam's race.
It was indeed an awful sight to see;
And oft, I fear, for what my love hath done,
As voucher of thy sweet communion
In thy sweet *Saviour's* blessed mystery.
Would I might give thee back, my little one,
But half the good which I derive from thee.

XXX

TO A DEAF AND DUMB LITTLE GIRL

Like a loose island on the wide expanse,
Unconscious floating on the fickle sea,
Herself her all, she lives in privacy;
Her waking life as lonely as a trance,
Doom'd to behold the universal dance,
And never hear the music which expounds
The solemn step, coy slide, the merry bounds,
The vague, mute language of the countenance.
In vain for her I smooth my antic rhyme;
She cannot hear it. All her little being
Concentred in her solitary seeing—
What can she know of beauty or sublime?
And yet methinks she looks so calm and good,
God must be with her in her solitude!

[1] This sonnet was addressed to Hartley Coleridge's 'dear little God-daughter, Caroline Green'.

XXXI

TO LILLY

RIGHT merry lass, thy overweening joy
Turns an old man into a merry boy.
One hour with thee pays off the long arrears,
The heavy debt of almost fifty years.
Oft have I view'd that lake so beautiful,
And felt its quiet power, benign, to lull
The inward being to a soft repose;
Patient, yet not forgetful of the woes
That are the heritage of mortal breath,
As if one note divided life and death.
But thou, sweet maid, with ready mirtn dost fill
The wide survey of water, wood, and hill.
I feel a pulse of pleasure newly born,
And scarce believe that 'man was made to mourn'.

XXXII

I SAW thee in the beauty of thy spring,
And then I thought how blest the man shall be
That shall persuade thy maiden modesty
To hearken to his fond soliciting.
Thou wert so fair, so exquisite a thing,
I thought the very dust on which thy feet
Had left their mark exhaled a scent more sweet
Than honey-dew dropt from an angel's wing.
I see thee now a matron and a mother,
And I, alas! am old before my day.
Both to myself and thee I owe another—
A holier passion, a devouter lay.
Each spark of earthly fire I now must smother,
And wish for nought for which I dare not pray.

---

¹ This sonnet was addressed to Mrs. Isaac Green. While she was still Caroline Ibbetson, Hartley Coleridge had been deeply attached to her and he continued to admire her after her marriage.

XXXIII

Written on the 29th of May, 1847, while Dora Quillinan was lying on her death-bed.

WELL, this is really like the month of May,
The merry May of which we used to hear,
Big with the promise of the coming year!
The apple-trees their rosy bloom display,
The flow'rets, many-hued, that line the way,
Long-soak'd with rain and chill'd with bitter blast,
Look happy now, like maidens, that at last
Are to be wedded, after long delay.
Oh! that the joy, the fragrance, and the bloom,
That bid all life and even poor man be glad,
Might waft a breath of comfort to the room
Where she lies smitten, yet not wholly sad,
Waiting with frame immortal to be clad,
In patient expectation of her doom!

XXXIV

PRAYER

THERE is an awful quiet in the air,
And the sad earth, with moist imploring eye,
Looks wide and wakeful at the pondering sky,
Like Patience slow subsiding to Despair.
But see, the blue smoke as a voiceless prayer,
Sole witness of a secret sacrifice,
Unfolds its tardy wreaths, and multiplies
Its soft chameleon breathings in the rare
Capacious ether,—so it fades away,
And nought is seen beneath the pendent blue,
The undistinguishable waste of day.
So have I dream'd—oh, may the dream be true!—
That praying souls are purged from mortal hue,
And grow as pure as He to whom they pray.

XXXV

PRAYER

BE not afraid to pray—to pray is right.
Pray, if thou canst, with hope; but ever pray,
Though hope be weak, or sick with long delay;
Pray in the darkness, if there be no light.
Far is the time, remote from human sight,
When war and discord on the earth shall cease;
Yet every prayer for universal peace
Avails the blessed time to expedite.
Whate'er is good to wish, ask that of Heaven,
Though it be what thou canst not hope to see:
Pray to be perfect, though material leaven
Forbid the Spirit so on earth to be;
But if for any wish thou darest not pray,
Then pray to God to cast that wish away.

XXXVI

JESUS PRAYING

LUKE VI, 12

He sought the mountain and the loneliest height,
For He would meet his Father all alone,
And there, with many a tear and many a groan,
He strove in prayer throughout the long, long night.
Why need He pray, who held by filial right,
O'er all the world alike of thought and sense,
The fullness of his Sire's omnipotance?
Why crave in prayer what was his own by might?
Vain is the question,—Christ was man in deed,
And being man, his duty was to pray.
The Son of God confess'd the human need,
And doubtless ask'd a blessing every day,
Nor ceases yet for sinful man to plead,
Nor will, till heaven and earth shall pass away.

XXXVII

HAGAR

Lone in the wilderness, her child and she,
Sits the dark beauty, and her fierce-eyed boy;
A heavy burden, and no winsome toy
To such as her, a hungry babe must be.
A slave without a master—wild, not free,
With anger in her heart! and in her face
Shame for foul wrong and undeserved disgrace,
Poor Hagar mourns her lost virginity!
Poor woman, fear not—God is everywhere;
Thy silent tears, thy thirsty infant's moan,
Are known to Him, whose never-absent care
Still wakes to make all hearts and souls his own;
He sends an angel from beneath his throne
To cheer the outcast in the desert bare.

XXXVIII

SUNDAY

Thou blessed day! I will not call thee last,
Nor Sabbath,—last nor first of all the seven,
But a calm slip of intervening heaven,
Between the uncertain future and the past;
As in a stormy night, amid the blast,
Comes ever and anon a truce on high,
And a calm lake of pure and starry sky
Peers through the mountainous depth of clouds amass'd.
Sweet day of prayer! e'en they whose scrupulous dread
Will call no other day, as others do,
Might call thee Sunday without fear or blame;
For thy bright morn deliver'd from the dead
Our Sun of Life, and will for aye renew
To faithful souls the import of thy name.

1843.

XXXIX
CONTINUATION

THE ancient Sabbath was an end,—a pause,—
A stillness of the world; the work was done!
But ours commemorates a work begun.
Why, then, subject the new to antique laws?
The ancient Sabbath closed the week, because
The world was finish'd. Ours proclaims the sun,
Its glorious saint, alert its course to run.
Vanguard of days! escaped the baffled jaws
Of slumberous dark and death,—so fitly first
Is Sunday placed before the secular days;
Unmeetly clad in weeds, with arms reversed,
To trail in sullen thought by silent ways.
Like the fresh dawn, or rose-bud newly burst,
So let our Sabbath wear the face of praise!

1843.

XL
THE SOUL

Is not the body more than meat? The soul
Is something greater than the food it needs.
Prayers, sacraments, and charitable deeds,
They realise the hours that onward roll
Their endless way 'to kindle or control'.
Our acts and words are but the pregnant needs
Of future being, when the flowers and weeds,
Local and temporal, in the vast whole
Shall live eternal. Nothing ever dies!
The shortest smile that flits across a face,
Which lovely grief hath made her dwelling-place,
Lasts longer than the earth or visible skies!
It is an act of God, whose acts are truth,
And vernal still in everlasting youth.

XLI

PRIVILEGES

Good is it to be born in Christian land,
Within the hearing of sweet Sabbath bells,
To con our letters in the book that tells
How God vouchsafed His creatures to command.
How once He led His chosen by the hand,
Presenting to their young and opening sense
Such pictures of His dread Omnipotence,
As all could see, though none might understand.
Oh! good it is to dwell with Christian folk,
Where even the deaf may see, the blind may hear,
The words that Paul endited, Jesus spoke,
By book or preacher shewn to eye or ear,
Where Gospel truth is rife as song of birds—
Familiar in our mouths as 'household words'.

XLII

'*MULTUM DILEXIT*'

She sat and wept beside His feet; the weight
Of sin oppress'd her heart; for all the blame,
And the poor malice of the worldly shame,
To her was past, extinct, and out of date,
Only the *sin* remain'd—the leprous state;
She would be melted by the heat of love,
By fires far fiercer than are blown to prove
And purge the silver ore adulterate.
She sat and wept, and with her untress'd hair
Still wiped the feet she was so blest to touch;
And He wiped off the soiling of despair
From her sweet soul, because she loved so much.
I am a sinner, full of doubts and fears,
Make me a humble thing of love and tears.

1848.

XLIII

TO A FRIEND
SUFFERING UNDER A RECENT BEREAVEMENT

THINK not, my friend, my heart or hand are cold
Because I do not, and I cannot, weep.
Too sudden was the knowledge of the woe,
And it requires some time, some thoughtful pause,
Ere we believe what but too well we know.
Some men are lesson'd long in sorrow's school,
And serve a long apprenticeship to grief,
So, when the ill day comes, their minds are clad
In funeral garments. Death came here at once,
Like the sun's setting in the level sea;
No meek, pale, warning, melancholy eve,
Wean'd the fond eyesight from the joyous day;
'Twas full-orb'd day, and then 'twas total night—
Sad night for us, but better day for her.
Well may'st thou mourn, but mourn not without hope;
Thou art not one, I know, that can believe
A pausing pulse, an intermitted breath,
Or aught that can to mortal flesh befall,
Can turn to nothing any way of God,
Or frustrate one good purpose of our Lord.
She was a purpose of her great Creator,
Begun on earth, and well on earth pursued,
Now in the heaven of heavens consummate,
Or only waiting 'till the destined day,
The flower and glory of her consummation.

XLIV

With the last day of the first month, I conclude this miscellaneous chaos of sense and nonsense. Like a candle lighted at both ends, my book is exhausted at the centre. It was begun when I stood high in the world, proud but not glad of academic honours, with all the material, but, alas! without the moral of happiness. Its conclusion finds me a beggar, bankrupt in estate, in love, in friendship, and, worst of all, in self-esteem. Yet the faith with which it was commenced has ripened into certainty, and the sad knowledge of what I am feelingly informs me what I might have been.

This day, too, I beheld the first snowdrop, the earliest primrose. Nature begins to revive, and why should not I commence a new year from this day?

[From a memorandum, dated 1827, in one of Hartley Coleridge's notebooks.]

A WOEFUL thing it is to find
No trust secure in weak mankind;
But ten-fold woe betide the elf
Who knows not how to trust himself.

What then remains? Can oath or vow,
Or formal protest aid me?
Ah! no, for if I make them now,
Next week they will upbraid me:
For what I am, oh! shame and sorrow,
I cannot hope to be to-morrow.

If I am weak, yet God is strong,
If I am false, yet God is true.
Old things are past, or right or wrong,
And every day that comes is new.
To-morrow then fresh hope may bring,
And rise with healing on its wing.

1827.

XLV

LINES

Oh for a man, I care not what he be,
A lord or labourer, so his soul be free,
Who had one spark of that celestial fire
That did the Prophets of old time inspire,
When Joel made the mystic trumpet cry,
When Jeremiah raised his voice on high,
And rapt Isaiah felt his great heart swell
With all the sins and woes of Israel!
Not such am I,—a petty man of rhyme,
Nursed in the softness of a female time.
From May of life to Autumn have I trod
The earth, not quite unconscious of my God;
But apter far to recognize His power
In sweet perfection of a pencill'd flower,
A kitten's gambols, or a birdie's nest,
A baby sleeping on its mother's breast,
Than in the fearful passages of life,—
The battle-field, the never ceasing strife
Of policy that ever would be wise,
Dissecting truth into convenient lies,—
The gallows, or the press-gang, or the press,—
The poor man's pittance, ever less and less,—
The dread magnificence of ancient crime.
Or the mean mischief of the present time.
Yet there is something in my heart that would
Become a witness to eternal good.
Woe to the man that wastes his wealth of mind,
And leaves no legacy to human kind!
I love my country well,—I love the hills,
I love the valleys and the vocal rills;
But most I love the men, the maids, the wives,
The myriad multitude of human lives.

XLVI
SONG

—————

In June, when the rose-buds
  Are ready to blow,
We love something in them
  Far more than we know.
When we look on a baby,
  We love what we see—
We love what it may be,
  And hope it will be.

But my love, sweet Mary,
  For thee, as I know,
Is a rose-bud untimely
  That never will blow.
My love is a baby,
  No blessing will crave,
But come, love, however,
  And smile on its grave.

XLVII
TO — — — —

—————

If I were young as I have been,
And you were only sweet fifteen,
I would address you as a goddess,
Write 'loyal cantos' to your boddice,
Would wish myself your cap, your shoe,
Or any thing, that near to you.
But I am old, and you, my fair,
Are somewhat older than you were.
A lover's language in your hearing
Would sound like irony and jeering.
Once you were fair to all that see,
Now you are only fair to me.

XLVIII

ANGELS have wings? Well, let them grow—
May it be long before *you* know
  Whether they have or not.
But geese have wings, and quills as good,
Perhaps, as wings of angels could
  Supply—could they be got.

But oh! dear lady, why contrive
To make the vainest man alive
  Conceited more than ever:
I will not call these pens divine,
But certain they were pens of thine,
  And that's enough, however.

XLIX

TO GOODY TWO SHOES[1]

Ah, little Goody! I have known thee long,
   And feel it strange to call thee Lady Jones.
Art thou as happy mid the bowing throng.
   As when thou heard'st thy *two shoes* on the stones?
Sole sound of comfort that could reach thy heart,
When thy companion child must needs depart.

[1] In one of his notebooks Hartley Coleridge writes most charmingly concerning Charles Lamb's gift of *Goody Two Shoes* and kindred books: 'I am ill at dates, and cannot remember the year—either *anno Domini* or *ætatis suæ*—when Charles Lamb despatched from London to Keswick a precious pacquet consisting of little books of the Right New Baby Cut—procured after long search, with some difficulty and the sneer of the Shopman.—It must needs seem ungrateful, when artists of merit are employed to illustrate children's books with engravings that would not have disgraced a quarto—and the backs themselves imitate monkish illumination, to say that I prefer the old wooden sculptures, rather symbolic than imitative—and the square-covers—gilt in tempting resemblance to gingerbread; yet I do wish I could get *Goody Two Shoes* as originally written—for the modern abridgements are vile—in the same square volume, with the same gilt covers, and the same queer prints, in which I read it with so much difficulty (for I was very backward in my reading) and so many curious misapprehensions of its meaning—for it is all for children. What heart, what knowledge, what true piety there is in that little story! It is said to have been written by Goldsmith— and I believe it. . . . To be sure the conclusion is bad enough—where Goody becomes Lady Jones—but all the liker Goldsmith for that. What can be clumsier than the conclusion of the *Vicar of Wakefield*? But I care nothing about conclusions. A book must end somehow—with marriage—or death—or a nunnery. But the characters we love, the scenes we dwell in, end not, change not—die not. Robinson Crusoe is on the Island still, sometimes with poor Friday and sometimes all alone. . . . Here is another prosing excursion grown out of a book with a gilt cover. I had another of the same size and shape, both given me by dear Charles Lamb—*Mother Goose's Tales—Little Red Riding Hood—Toads and Diamonds—Blue Beard—The Sleeping Beauty—Puss in Boots*—(I never could think that *Puss in Boots* was true) —*The Ogre and Tom Thumb*—which I once converted ihto a very bad Pantomime—and the *Discreet Princess* which I was never tired of hearing. I have never read it since I was christened—that is—since I was seven—. . . . I remember my good godmother reading it to me again and again.—She was an excellent reader—I see her now in her close cap, black triangular kerchief, and spectacles, I hear her elderly but mellow voice, the echo of kindness—there are few such old maids. Were I to lose all the good in heart and head that I derived from her—I should have little left. It was long before I would let her finish *Blue Beard*. . . . my heart is calmer, happier, more pious whenever I think of these stories—they make me wish to be innocent again—to be worthy of being loved as I was when they were read to me by my godmother Wilsy. They carry me back to my childhood and the journey is as salutary to the soul as nature. . . . The first poem I remember reading myself was Wordsworth's "We are Seven." I was a slow reader—and asked so many questions that it was no pleasant task to teach me. I could not understand the philosophic drift of the tale, nor can I yet perceive why it was selected for a lesson—but the image of the little girl sitting with her little porringer by the graves of her brother and sister took up its abode in my imagination—never to depart. . . . A picture, whether in verse or prose, interested me much more than a series of events—I was moreover exceedingly retrospective."

Thy lamb, thy raven, and thy box of letters,
   Thy love for all the tribes of earth and air,
Thy shrewd odd sayings, apt to make thy betters,
   Or folks so call'd, look round with wondrous stare
And deeper minds reflect on wisdom given
To fortune's waifs by compensating Heaven;—

All these, to curious childhood dear, as new,
   Retain a value to the satiate age,
And press full oft before the inward view
   Of souls long strangers to the brief square page,
The tinsell'd covers, and the strange old pictures
That served our ancestors instead of lectures.

I've trembled with thee in the church so cold,
   And fearful in its soundless solitude.
What place so dreary as deserted fold,
   Where few hours past the shepherd wise and good
Had spoke the words that take the sting from death,
And change our human tears to wells of faith?

But more of fear and more of pain was thine,
   And short and smother'd was thy sweet breath, when
A little musty hay, a narrow line
   Of darkness, parted thee from evil men,
With horrid whisper plotting crime and plunder,
Mocking with mutter'd oaths the awful thunder.

O neighbourhood unmeet for one like thee;
   Yet out of evil, maids whose minds are right,
As thine was in its sweet simplicity,
   Draw blessings for themselves; celestial light
Beams on the weakest in extreme distresses—
Assurance, where proud prudence hardly guesses.

Such wert thou, Goody, in thy childish days,
   And though, no doubt, thou didst grow old in time,
And wert a spinster much deserving praise,
   That praise I will not speak in prose or rhyme;
For rather I'd believe thee tripping still
With Ralph the Raven, and with Baa-Lamb Bill.

L

TO A CAT

NELLY, methinks, 'twixt thee and me
There is a kind of sympathy;
And could we interchange our nature,—
If I were cat, thou human creature,—
I should, like thee, be no great mouser,
And thou, like me, no great composer;
For, like thy plaintive mews, my muse
With villainous whine doth fate abuse,
Because it hath not made me sleek
As golden down on Cupid's cheek;
And yet thou canst upon the rug lie,
Stretch'd out like snail, or curl'd up snugly,
As if thou wert not lean or ugly;
And I, who in poetic flights
Sometimes complain of sleepless nights,
Regardless of the sun in heaven,
Am apt to dose till past eleven,—
The world would just the same go round
If I were hang'd and thou wert drown'd;
There is one difference, 'tis true,—
Thou dost not know it, and I do.

LI

TO WILLIAM WORDSWORTH
ON HIS SEVENTY-FIFTH BIRTHDAY

HAPPY the year, the month, that finds alive
A worthy man in health at seventy-five.
Were he a man no further known than loved,
And but for unremember'd deeds approved,
A gracious boon it were from God to earth
To leave that good man by his humble hearth.
But if the man be one whose virtuous youth,
Loving all Nature, was in love with truth;
And with the fervour of religious duty
Sought in all shapes the very form of beauty;—
Feeling the current of the tuneful strain,
Joy in his heart, and light upon his brain,
Knew that the gift was given, and not in vain;
Whose careful manhood never spared to prune
What the rash growth of youth put forth too soon;
Too wise to be ashamed to grow more wise;
Culling the truth from specious fallacies:—
Then may the world rejoice to find alive
So good, so great a man, at seventy-five.

LII

THE FOURTH BIRTHDAY

FOUR years, long years, with mighty matters rife
　　To thee, sweet boy, though brief and bare to me,
Complete the computation of thy life,
　　And far out-date thy little memory.

How many tears have dropp'd since thou wert born,
　　Some on the cradle, some upon the grave!
Yet having thee, thy father, not forlorn,
　　Felt he had something yet of God to crave.

For who hath aught to love, and loves aright,
　　Will never in the darkest strait despair;
For out of love exhales a living light,
　　A light that speaks—a light whose voice is prayer.

Sorrow hath been within thy dwelling, child,
　　Yet sorrow hath not touch'd thy delicate bloom;
So, the low floweret in Arabian wild
　　Grows in the sand, nor fades in the simoom.

What thou hast lost thou know'st not, canst not know,
　　Too young to wonder when thy elders moan;
Thou haply think'st that adult eyes can flow
　　With tears as quick and transient as thine own.

The swift adoption of an infant's love
　　Gives to thy heart all infant hearts require;
Unfelt by thee, the mortal shaft that clove
　　In twain thy duty, left thy love entire.

Ne'er be thy birthday as a day unblest,
　　Which thou or thine might wish had never been;
But in thine age, a quiet day of rest,
　　A Sabbath, holy, thoughtful, and serene.

1837.

LIII

SUMMER RAIN

THICK lay the dust, uncomfortably white,
In glaring mimicry of Arab sands.
The woods and mountains slept in hazy light;
The meadows look'd athirst and tawny tann'd;
The little rills had left their channels bare,
With scarce a pool to witness what they were;
And the shrunk river gleam'd 'mid oozy stones,
That stared like any famish'd giant's bones.

Sudden the hills grew black, and hot as stove
The air beneath; it was a toil to be.
There was a growling as of angry Jove,
Provoked by Juno's prying jealousy—
A flash—a crash—the firmament was split,
And down it came in drops—the smallest fit
To drown a bee in fox-glove bell conceal'd;
Joy fill'd the brook, and comfort cheer'd the field.

LIV

THE ANEMONE

WHO would have thought a thing so slight,
So frail a birth of warmth and light,
A thing as weak as fear or shame,
Bearing thy weakness in thy name,—
Who would have thought of finding thee,
Thou delicate Anemone,
Whose faintly tinted petals may
By any wind be torn away,
Whose many anthers with their dust,
And the dark purple dome their centre,
When winter strikes, soon as *it likes*,
Will quit their present rest, and must
Hurry away on wild adventure?
What power has given thee to outlast
The pelting rain, the driving blast;
To sit upon thy slender stem,
A solitary diadem,
Adorning latest autumn with
A relic sweet of vernal pith?

Oh Heaven! if,—as faithful I believe,—
Thou wilt the prayer of faithful love receive,
Let it be so with me! I was a child,
A child of large belief; though forward, wild,
Gladly I listened to the holy word,
And deem'd my little prayers by God were heard.
All things I loved, however strange or odd,
As deeming all things were beloved by God.
In youth and manhood's careful sultry hours,
The garden of my youth bore many flowers
That now are faded; but my early faith,
Though thinner far than vapour, spectre, wraith,
Lighter than aught the rude wind blows away,
Has yet outlived the rude tempestuous day,
And may remain, a witness of the spring,
A sweet, a holy, and a lovely thing;
The promise of another spring to me,
My lovely, lone, and lost Anemone!

Ambleside, November.

LV

THE LILY OF THE VALLEY

SOME flowers there are that rear their heads on high,
The gorgeous products of a burning sky,
That rush upon the eye with garish bloom,
And make the senses drunk with high perfume.
Not such art thou, sweet Lily of the Vale!
So lovely, small, and delicately pale,—
We might believe, if such fond faith were ours,
As sees humanity in trees and flowers,
That thou wert once a maiden, meek and good,
That pined away beneath her native wood
For very fear of her own loveliness,
And died of love she never would confess.

May 24, 1846.

LVI

'When Messrs. Hawes and Fellowes ascended Mont Blanc in July, 1827,
they observed a butterfly near the summit. Mr. C. Shewell saw two
crimson moths at nearly the same elevation.'—*New Monthly Magazine.*

WHO would have thought, upon this icy cliff,
　　Where never ibex bounded
　　Nor foot of chamois sounded,
Where never soaring hippogriff
　　Hath lighted, unless truly,
　　To this exalted Thule,
He carried the thoughts of a metaphysician,
Or theory of an electrician—
Who would have dream'd of seeing thee,
Softest of summer's progeny?
What art thou seeking?　What hast thou lost,
That before the throne of eternal frost
Thou art come to spread the crimson wing,
Thou pretty fluttering thing?
Art thou too fine for the world below?
Hast thou too soon over lived thy spring?
　　And now hast sworn
　　To live forlorn
An anchorite in a cave of snow?

Or dost thou fancy, as many have done,
That because the hill-top is nearest the Sun,
   The Sun loves better the ne'er-thawn ice,
That does nothing but tell him that he is bright
And dissect like a prism his braided light—
   Than the gardens of bloom and the groves of spice?
Dost imagine the bright one his mystery shrouds
In a comfortless mantle of sleet-driving clouds?
   Alas! he never loved this place;
   It bears no token of his grace,
But many a scar of the season's lash
And stigmatic brand of the sulphurous flash.
'Tis better to dwell amid corn-fields and flowers
Or even the weeds of this world of ours,
Than to leave the green vale and the sunny slope,
To seek the cold cliff with a desperate hope.
   Flutter he, flutter he, high as he will,
   A Butterfly is but a Butterfly still.
And 'tis better for us to remain as we are
In the lowly valley of duty and care,
Than lonely to stray to the heights above,
Where is nothing to do, and nothing to love.

LVII

THE DESERTED CHURCH

A prophecy, the fulfilment of which the writer never wishes to see.[1]

AFTER long travail on my pilgrimage,
I sat me down beside an aged heap,
For so it seem'd, with one square shatter'd keep,
Pensively frowning on the wrecks of age.
The river there, as at its latest stage,
Sinks in the verdure of its Sunday sleep,
And sings an under-song for them that weep
O'er the sad blots in life's too open page.
I look'd within, but all within was cold!
The walls were mapp'd with isles of dusky damp,
The long stalls look'd irreverently old,
The rush-strewn aisle was like a wither'd swamp,
And mark'd with loitering foot's unholy tramp;
The chancel floor lay thick with sluggish mould.
Hark! do you hear the dull unfrequent knell,
Survivor sad of many a merry peal,
Whose Sabbath music wont to make us feel
Our spirits mounting with its joyous swell,
That scaled the height, that sunk into the dell?
Now lonely, lowly swinging to and fro,
It warns a scatter'd flock e'en yet to go,
And take a sip of the deserted well.
And, dost thou hear?—then, hearing, long endure.
The Gospel sounds not now so loud and bold
As once it did. Some lie in sleep secure,
And many faint because their love is cold;
But never doubt that God may still be found,
Long as one bell sends forth a Gospel sound!

[1] Though Derwent Coleridge printed this as one poem, it is really composed of
two sonnets.

LVIII

WYTHEBURN CHAPEL AND HOSTEL

Here, traveller, pause and think, and duly think
    What happy, holy thoughts may heavenward rise,
Whilst thou and thy good steed together drink
    Beneath this little portion of the skies.

See! on one side, a humble house of prayer,
    Where Silence dwells, a maid immaculate,
Save when the Sabbath and the priest are there,
    And some few hungry souls for manna wait.

Humble it is and meek and very low,
    And speaks its purpose by a single bell;
But God Himself, and He alone, can know
    If spiry temples please Him half so well.

Then see the world, the world in its best guise,
    Inviting thee its bounties to partake;
Dear is the Sign's old time-discolour'd dyes,
    To weary trudger by the long black lake.

And pity 'tis that other studded door,
    That looks so rusty right across the way,
Stands not always as was the use of yore,
    That whoso passes may step in and pray.

Betwixt prayer and provender, the road is driven
    The slave of every wheel of all men's tread,
Hard by, Helvellyn—steep as wall of heaven—
    May help thy thought to scale from the nag's head.[1]

---

[1] On the manuscript copy of this poem Hartley Coleridge wrote: 'The thought very imperfectly worked out; worth hammering at."

LIX

A GRACE

SWEETEST Lord! that wert so blest
On thy sweetest mother's breast,
Give to every new-born baby
Food that needs—as good as may be.
Jesus! Lord, who long obey'd
The sainted sire, the Mother Maid,
Teach my young heart to submit,—
Deign thyself to govern it.
Babe, and boy, and youth, and man,
All make up the mighty plan;
And these the Saviour sanctified,
For He was all—and then He died.
Whate'er He gives us we may take,
But still receive it for His sake.
But might the prayer within my breast
Make others blest, as I am blest;
And might my joy in thanking Thee
Make for all hungry souls a plea;
Then would I praise and Thee adore,
And ever thank Thee, more and more
Rejoicing, if Thou would'st but bless
Thy creatures for my thankfulness.

LX

CHAUCER

How wayward oft appears the poet's fate,
Who still is born too early or too late!
If a bold, fond, imaginative age,
Instinct with amorous, and with martial rage,
Enact more wonders than the mind conceives,
And all that fancy can devise believes,
Produce a man by natural right a bard,
To whom long thought, and chance perplex'd and hard,
And books and men, and pensive cells and courts,
And politic lore, and trade, and knightly sports,
And, more than all, his own repented sin
Have shown the outer world and that within;—
The fleeting language, to its trust untrue,
Vext by the jarring claims of old and new,
Defeats his beauty, makes his sense the fee
Of a blind, guessing, blundering glossary.
Thus CHAUCER, quaintly clad in antique guise,
With unfamiliar mien scares modern eyes.
No doubt he well invented—nobly felt—
But, O ye Powers! how monstrously he spelt.
His syllables confound our critic men,
Who strive in vain to find exactly ten;
And waste much learning to reduce his songs
To modish measurement of shorts and longs.
His language, too, unpolish'd and unfixt,
Of Norman, Saxon, Latin, oddly mixt—
Such words might please [th'] uneducated ears
That hail'd the blaring trumpets of Poictiers.
They shared the sable Edward's glee and glory,
And, like his conquests, they were transitory.
Then how shall such old-fashion'd lingo cope
With polish, elegance, and Mister Pope?

Yet, thou true Poet! let no judgment wrong
Thy rich, spontaneous, many colour'd song;
Just mirror of a bold, ambitious age,
In passion furious, in reflection sage!—
An age of gorgeous sights and famous deeds,
And virtue more than peace admits or needs;
When shiver'd lances were our ladies' sport,
And love itself assumed a lofty port;
When every beast, and bird, and flower, and tree,
Convey'd a meaning and a mystery;
And men in all degrees, sorts, ranks, and trades,
Knights, Palmers, Scholars, Wives, devoted Maids,
In garb, and speech, and manners, stood confest
To outward view, by hues and signs exprest,
And told their state and calling by their vest.

LXI

SHAKESPEARE

SHAKESPEARE, what art thou? Could'st thou rise again
To praise thyself, thy praise were old and vain;
Thy highest flight would sink beneath thy due;
Thy own invention would find nothing new.
In the whole orb of nature that thou art,
Complete in essence, and distinct in part;
No theme, no topic, and no simile,
But busy men have stolen in praise of thee.
Then let thy cumbrous critics keep their shelves;
We find thy truest comment in ourselves.
In thee our thoughts find utterance, and combine
Their airy substance with those thoughts of thine.
By thee our feelings all are judged, acquitted,
Reproved, condemn'd, with seemly action fitted.
What chance, or change, affection, or the faith
Of hope and fear, the benison or scathe
Of Fortune infinite can make of man,—
What man has been since first the world began,
Thou well hast shown. One task alone remains,
One great adventure for succeeding brains;
The golden branch upon the mystic tree,
Unpluck'd, to show—man as he ought to be.

LXII

DONNE

BRIEF was the reign of pure poetic truth;
A race of thinkers next, with rhymes uncouth,
And fancies fashion'd in laborious brains,
Made verses heavy as o'erloaded wains.
Love was their theme, but love that dwelt in stones,
Or charm'd the stars in their concentric zones;
Love that did erst the nuptial bond conclude
'Twixt immaterial form and matter rude;
Love that was riddled, sphered, transacted, spelt,
Sublimed, projected, everything but felt.
Or if in age, in orders, or the cholic,
They damn'd all loving as a heathen frolic;
They changed their topic, but in style the same,
Adored their maker as they wooed their dame.
Thus DONNE, not first, but greatest of the line,
Of stubborn thoughts a garland thought to twine;
To his fair Maid brought cabalistic posies,
And sung quaint ditties of metempsychosis;
'Twists iron poker into true love-knots',
Coining hard words, not found in polyglots.

LXIII

'I HAVE written my name on water'.
And if thou hast, where could'st thou write it better
Than on the feeder of all lives that live?
The tide, the stream, will bear away the letter,
And all that formal is and fugitive:
Still shall thy Genius be a vital power,
Feeding the root of many a beauteous flower.

PART III
UNPUBLISHED AND UNCOLLECTED POEMS

I

FULL well I know—my Friends—ye look on me
A living spectre of my Father dead—
Had I not borne his name, had I not fed
On him, as one leaf trembling on a tree,
A woeful waste had been my minstrelsy—
Yet have I sung of maidens newly wed
And I have wished that hearts too sharply bled
Should throb with less of pain, and heave more free
By my endeavour. Still alone I sit
Counting each thought as Miser counts a penny,
Wishing to spend my penny-worth of wit
On antic wheel of fortune like a Zany:
You love me for my sire, to you unknown,
Revere me for his sake, and love me for my own.[1]

[1] Published in *Hartley Coleridge: His Life and Work*, p. 185.

II

CHRISTMAS DAY, 1840

The following sonnet was contained in a letter to Derwent Coleridge, concluding: 'Give my best love and compliments to Mama, but stay—I must write her a sonnet—for God knows——'.

Now is the Time, as old Tradition tells,
When the untainted Mother—second Eve
Brought forth the God—through whom we all believe,
That spiritual God—that in the good heart dwells—
Oh—Mother, listening to the Christmas bells—
Blithe ringing for the joyous holy day
I very gladly would evoke a lay
That would be light in thine heart's inmost cells.
Oh—dearest Mother, I have lived too long,
If you have quite forgot the joyous song
With which we used to greet this holy time—
Sad is it now to think—but so it is—
Our Mother from her once beloved Quizz[1]—
Can have no Christmas gift—except a rhime.

---

[1] In an unpublished fragment Hartley Coleridge gives an *Autobiography of a Quizz: Can the Ethiopian change his skin, or the Leopard his spots?*
'Next to being born a Queen, the greatest misfortune in the World is to be born a Quizz. It is infinitely better to squint or stammer, to be hunch-back'd, club-footed, hare-lipped, to be blind, deaf, dumb, or an idiot, anything in fact, but a rascal, than to be a Quizz. Even insanity, when it amounts to that degree which is irresponsible and unconscious of itself, is a lighter infliction. All other natural infirmities are to good minds, objects of pity, and in some measure, of respect. *Sacra res miser est.* All other calamities are referred to nature, or to providence, or, even if they be the allotted penalty of guilt, he who is conscious of a single sin, will not throw the first stone. If the offence were wilful, the punishment is known to be involuntary, and therefore, not excluded from compassion. The Quizz alone is condemned as wilfully miserable, for miserable indeed he is, who is out of the pale of human sympathy, who may have well-wishers, but neither friends nor lovers—who is an inexplicable riddle to his fellow-creatures, whose thoughts and feelings have no intelligible language, who is subject to an alien law that cannot be repeated, as strange in the wide world as if he were, like the Mosasaurus and Megatherium, a relic of a perished system, or dropped, like a selenite from the moon.

III

Oh—why, my Brother, are we thus apart
Never to meet, but in abortive dreams,
That ever break away, in shuddering screams,
Leaving a panting vacancy of heart?
How often from my restless bed I start
Thinking to find thee—not yet half awake
Till sergeant Memory, with an angry shake
Tells me where I am; while alas! thou art
Conversing sweetly with night-warbling thought,
That makes thy every pulse an answered prayer
For her, the dear bird in thy meshes caught
Whom seeing not, thou feel'st to be most fair.
Come gently on my visions, bless my sight,
Let me not always be an Anchorite.

[*Dale End, October* 6, 1835.]

IV

Five senses hath the bounteous Lord bestow'd,
Inlets of knowledge, and free ports of joys.
Mercurial hearing, that creates the ode
And sweet song—from the chaos of brute noise.
The touch that melts upon an infant's neck,
The taste, approving English hospitality,
And reminiscent smell to wake or check
Thoughts of old time, and bowery sociality,
And sight, of senses most intelligent
And deepest dwelling in the central mind
With the past hoards of form and hue content
And ofttimes mightiest in the outward blind.
What are they all, but talents from above
Blest for the souls that can believe and love?

1841.

V

Oh when I have a sovereign in my pocket
I cannot sit—my toes extempore dance
Gay as a limber son of merry France;
'Tis like grey hair enclose[d] in gilded locket
Whose gold and glass by contrast seem to mock it;
So momentary riches will enhance
The pride of Poverty, so high advance
The hope of man—but soon alas a docket—
Misfortune strikes, the obliterating sponge
Of fell reverse makes all our joys exhale.
Shall I in ocean take a fatal plunge
Or shall I with sixpenny worth of ale
Condole the sovereign spent—or get quite frisky
And just hibernify myself with whiskey?[1]

VI

TO BE PRESENTED TO PODALIRIUS—ON THE ANNIVERSARY OF HIS MARRIAGE (WEATHER PERMITTING)[2]

I wander'd forth, as I am wont, at morn
And felt a healing freshness in the air;
I breath'd in bliss and wondered where they were—
Those happy sprights, and where so newly born;
Heirs to the wealth of Amalthea's horn
They fill'd the day with bounty of their dower:
When lo! the holy fragrance of a flower
Constrain'd my feet into a brake of thorn.
I found a flower—I knew not how to name
A pale white flower, its stem erect and tall
But ever earthward droop'd its pensive head—
As if to worship that from which it came—
No mates it had—or it had lost them all,
Meek transmigration of the life unwed.

[1] From an original manuscript in the possession of Mr. Herbert Bell.
[2] In another copy Hartley Coleridge entitled this poem, 'The Flower and the Doves—or Single and Married Life'. This and the following sonnet were addressed to William Fell, who was for many years a physician in the Lake Country.

VII

CONTINUATION

I LEFT the thorn brake for I dared not cull
That flower recluse—The day rejoiced in light
And yet I deemed the world less beautiful,
Musing on that balm breathing anchorite.
Again I sought a thicket's dewy night,
And unawares a happy nest of Doves,
With callow babes to multiply their loves,
Started in softest fulgence on my sight.
Well be it with thee then—in lovely glade
Still sanctify thy body to a shade,
And die as thou hast lived, lone flower, alone.
I cannot deem thee holier or more blest
Than those sweet inmates of the homely nest
Whose goodness craves not, fears not, to be known.

VIII

INVOCATION TO SPRING

O SPRING—where art thou? Have we done thee wrong?
Art angry with us? Come, O come away,
The Sun is climbing; every lengthened day
Makes us almost lament the day so long,
While day by day untimely snow flakes throng
The cold dim atmosphere, beneath the grey
Uncomfortable sky. Think how poor May,
Thy darling, soon must pine and starve among
The unclad woods. A primrose here and there,
And here and there a venturous Celandine
Looks out for thee, and seems to wonder where
Are all their sisters sweet, and mates so fair,
That used to make the bosky banks so fine
And breathe fresh life into the virgin air.[1]

[1] 'N.B.—May was quite as ill-accommodated as the Sonneteer anticipated. Not an oak-leaf could be found to do honour to King Charles's day. The season doubtless sympathised with the declining state of the Royal Tar; and brightened immediately on the accession of our gracious Queen.' Note by Miss Briggs, to whom the sonnet was sent.

Sedbergh, April 1837.

IX

TIME was when I could weep; but now all care
Is gone—yet have I gazed 'till sense deceived
Almost assures me that her bosom heav'd;
And o'er those features—as the lightest air
On summer sea—Life play'd, did they but bear
One trace of Mind, faintly in sleep perceiv'd,
Wand'ring, from earthly impulse unreliev'd—
Through regions of Emotion, wild or fair.
Her mind is gone! and now, while over all
A ghastly dreaming quiet seems to lie,
All Sounds subdued to mournful harmony,
My heart is tranquil; sunk beyond the Call
Of Hope or Fear; and still must deeper fall,
Down—down with Time, till e'en remembrance die.[1]

X

ON THE RECEPTION OF THE DUC DE BORDEAUX

'ENGLAND, with all thy faults I love thee still',
And love thee most for this, that neither breed
Nor colour, party, rank or caste, or creed,
Restrains thy bold and hospitable will—
That faction's poison never yet could kill
The duteous heart, that owns the right of need;
Nor form of faith forbid to say 'God speed'
All that in thought that holy word fulfil.
Him that in freedom's cause in vain hath striven
To raise a prostrate nation from the dust
Conspiring despots ne'er shall force away
From Britain's shore; the prince whom change hath riven
From Palace home, is here in sacred trust;
The slave escaped, no Briton will betray.

[1] This sonnet may refer to Dorothy Wordsworth. From an original manuscript in the possession of Mr. J. K. Hudson. Published in *Temple Bar*, April 1903, p. 413.

XI

TO THOMAS CLARKSON

Long hast thou laboured, long, and very hard,
For human woes. 'Twas not thy cue to weep
And like an infant cry thyself to sleep.
Oh no; thy manly nature did discard
All lazy, soft emotions, that retard
The active will in its sublime intent;
All dreams, that slumbering in their self-content,
Are, as they boast themselves, their own reward.
From the great day of that all faithful Vow,[1].
That swore the trade in human flesh should cease,
To the full freedom of consummate Now,
Thou still hast seen thy blessed fame increase.
Woe to the men that would disturb thine age
And stop the last step of thy pilgrimage!

[1] 'In the summer of 1785 young Thomas Clarkson was riding to London on horseback. A few weeks previously he had won a Latin prize at Cambridge for an essay on the subject, *Anne liceat invitos in servitutem dare?* ("Is it lawful to make slaves of others against their will?") In the preparation of his essay he had become acquainted with the shocking inhumanity attendant upon slavery. The stories of brutality and degradation oppressed him. . . . As he rode along he wondered what could be done to remedy the evil. Someone must begin the task, someone willing to devote his life to it. Descending the long hill into Wades Mill, he dismounted and fell to his knees, seeking divine guidance. When he arose his mind was made up—he would henceforth dedicate himself to the cause of the suffering negroes.' Thomas Clarkson, *The Friend of Slaves*, p. 23.

Thenceforth Clarkson was almost exclusively concerned with the abolition cause—'the moral Steam-Engine, or the Giant with one idea,' Samuel Taylor Coleridge once called him—but his hopes were realized, and he lived to see the abolition of the slave trade in 1807 and of slavery in the West Indies in 1833.

XII

TO BESSY——

——————

I FEAR you think (when friends by fate are parted
Fraught evermore in fear) that I forget
The small snug parlour where so oft we met
And that wee garden gate whence I have started
Oft on my homeward pad—not quite deserted
Though wending lonely through the dark and wet.
Thy voice was in mine ear, thy hand was yet
Thrilling in mine and made me lion hearted.
Nor can the blessing ever pass to nought
Which thou, dear Bessy, gavest so kind and free,
When far beyond the wide Atlantic Sea
Thy soul with recent care and knowledge fraught
Had for the old world many a loving thought
And yet could spare a loving thought for me.—

Such as I have that give I unto thee—Silver and Gold have I not—I would I had, for then I would send you something better than this very shambling sonnet which nevertheless is all the Interest I can pay upon my long arrears incurred by your late dear letter. You know I am a ruminating animal (though Asses I believe do not chew the cud) therefore for goodness sake—your own goodness I mean—believe that I have been ruminating on your letter ever since it arrived—I wish I could return you half the pleasure I received from that sweet token of remembrance— but that can hardly be—of our common Love you have taken more with you than you have left behind— The mountains and Lakes indeed are pretty much as they were, very grim and November like at this present but the people are quite another Generation—very good people in their way but not half so genial as what we can remember. Death, my dear Bessy, has been very busy among us—Of the Lads with whom I grew up I am almost the sole survivor—I feel like an old withered tree such as you sometimes see standing in a new felled Coppice— because it was not worth cutting down—and of your fair co-mates is there one you will ever meet again till you all meet in Heaven?

They lived awhile that we and all might see
How good a thing a woman ought to be;
They lived on earth just long enough to prove
That Earth is blest with its Creator's love;
They died—and dying proved their holiest worth
For God loved them more than he loved the earth.

Nov. 4 or 5 [Postmark Nov. 5, 1840] for it is got into 'some sma' hour beyond the twal'—I am now a Resident at the Knabbe and the November Wind sounds shrill from the dark firs of the Islands of Rydal. There is snow on Helvellyn and no fire in my grate but plenty in my pipe—I wish I had a magic glass to show you—all I hope fast asleep—Ere long the murky dawn of November will call out yon Cottage and its trees in ghost like dimness on the morning fog. If a bonfire blaze to-morrow drink to me.[1]

[1] The sonnet and the comments above formed part of a letter by Hartley Coleridge to an unknown correspondent.

XIII

ON WESTALL'S PICTURE, 'THE COTTAGE GIRL'

SURE it would seem a hard ingratitude
To Him that made you lovely as you are,
Should we lament that any thing so fair
Were born in state so poor—so wild and rude.
And yet forebodings sad will needs intrude
Of what may be the fate of one so bare,
So beautiful—Thy Grandam's pensive care
And even the stillness of thy own calm mood
Suggest a fear—May that all-gracious Lord
That led from Moab the young widowed Ruth
Be with thee still—for thou, sweet girl, in sooth
Hast need of all the guidance and the dread
Which an Almighty Father can afford
To maiden, wife, or woman widowed.

XIV

THE silent melody of thought that sings
A ceaseless requiem to the sainted Dead;
That so the sharp wound, hid within the Heart,
May grow a spot most finely sensible
To each good impress of the hand of God:
Till Death no longer seem'd a terrible thing,
But like a blithe and long wish'd Holy day
That frees the spirit, weary of the school
And discipline of Earth, once more to join
The friends and kindred of their happy home;
While the all-Father, with a look benign,
Praises the task, imperfect tho' it be,
And blesses all in their love and his own.[1]

---

[1] Published in Derwent Coleridge's *Memoir* of his brother, p. cxviii. These lines were included in a letter Hartley Coleridge wrote to his mother on the occasion of Coleridge's death. Cf. *Letters of Hartley Coleridge*, pp. 165–7.

XV

MARY FLEMING

DIED AUGUST, 1846. AGED 21 YEARS

Hush'd is the vale, yet ever and again
There comes a sigh as of o'ermastered pain;
The sky is clad in clouds, obscurely white
As garment of a female anchorite:
The voice we speak in is sedate and low,
Our wildest lads demurely walk and slow:
The clamorous wind holds in its noisy breath,
Awed by the presence of a holy death.

For she is dead that was of all approved,
And loving many was by many loved.
Small need, I ween, of that dull booming bell
Whose sad tautology is task'd to tell
What we all know—all, woefully, too well—
That she that wont to walk along the way
With step so light, yet firm, with heart so gay,
Yet self-possess'd—with form erect and tall,
And smiles that were a daily festival—
Now lies a model of inanimate earth,
Nor hears the sobs heaved by her desolate hearth,
Yet wears that look of patience that she wore
Through months of pain—still trying, often sore.

Yes, she was fair—and, better far, was good,
Most lovely in her early womanhood,—
Fair, yet not too fair for the busy life
And daily duties of a plain man's wife;
With just enough of scholarship to see
Both what she ought to do and ought to be,—
Full fitted seem'd she for the lot which heaven
In its benignant care to her had given.

But God, all-wise—and surely He knows best—
Decrees the maiden to be early blest.
We shall not see her, for she will not walk
In the cold moonshine, and she will not talk,
In the chill whistling of the midnight wind;
No buried treasure has she left behind;
No sin she did not upon earth confess
Obscures her hope of perfect blessedness.[1]
We shall not see her till—God grant we may
See her again—in God's eternal day![2]

[1] Accused of obscurity by the printer who issued a few copies of this poem for private circulation by the Fleming family, Hartley Coleridge answered: 'As to the lines which you characterise as obscure, I think you will find them clear enough if you recollect that according to the received belief of the *Ages of Faith*, two principal causes of a ghost's walking were the concealment of treasures or concealed sins. Except under these cases, persons who died from natural causes seldom or never became common-place bugga-boo ghosts, tho' eminent saints sometimes were permitted to appear in a glorified state to warn or console beloved survivors.'

[2] Published in *Temple Bar*, April, 1903, pp. 411–12.

XVI

ON THE LATE MRS. PRITT, FORMERLY MISS SCALES

A Christian Mother on a death-bed lies;
The life of nature flutters ere it dies
But faintly flutters, starts, and sinks again;
The life divine, with strong, impatient strain
Fights to be free, and struggles to be loose.
Yet mother's love obtains a moment's truce
For the last words, the latest, fondest prayer
That she shall mould in syllables of air,
And mid the pangs of an immortal birth
Thinks of the Babes that she must leave on earth.
She calls her husband to her death-bed side—
Few years ago she was a blushing bride
But never felt till now, the golden ring
So strict a bond, and such a holy thing.
Her words I will not try to put in verse;
To change them, were to change them for the worse.
To him her chosen from the sons of men
Her husband ever, most her husband then,
She left the nurture of her babes so sweet;
And one there was, she hoped again to meet
Ere many months were past, a tiny blossom
Untimely parted from maternal bosom;
And said, 'I will be but for a little while',
Then pain suppressed was melted to a smile,
So were her latest cares, like rose leaves shed
Upon the earth, three hours, and she was dead.

XVII

ON THE LATE MRS. GIBSON, FORMERLY MISS TWIST, A RELATION OF MR. GREENWOOD'S, GRASMERE

SHE was the darling of a happy house,
  And happy by the happiness she gave;
Bliss made her good and goodness beauteous;
  Merry she was, and active as a wave
That leaps in light and wears a glittering crest
When most beloved most fair and loveliest.

And sure that man must have been lov'd indeed,
  For whom she left her home, her native nest;
If ever wedding were on high decreed,
  A man and woman joined by God's behest,
Fond hope had said, 'this is the very pair',
And hope said true,—for so in truth they were.

But who could spy, when she, a serious bride
  Taming her girlish trip to matron pace,
Along the church way path was seen to glide,
  That death was omen'd in that vermeil face,
And the young heart that beat so joyous fast
So soon must beat in pain, and beat its last.

God gave her to the earth, a little while
  Made her a daughter, wife, and mother sweet
That she might prove His goodness with a smile,
  A human Angel,—mortal Paraclete,
But loving her beyond the common race
Recalls her quickly to her destin'd place.

XVIII

Walking beside Loughrigg Tarn, on a dreary wet Sunday towards the close of the revolutionary year 1848 I met a long train of carts, steaming umbrellas, women in Bombazine, and black silk bonnets of the old north country fashion—and neighbours in black suits some of which had seen more than one generation to the churchyard—and might see another, coats which if capable of thinking, might suppose departure the sole business of human life, so rarely had they been worn, but at a funeral——

These good people, as I soon recollected, were conveying from a Cottage in Loughrigg to Grasmere Church-yard the mortal remains of—Mackerett —a woman who had almost attained her hundredth year—dwelling most of her time in Loughrigg—and probably with very indistinct notions of the mighty changes that were taking place, even in her native vales, absorbed for half a century at least, in the one idea 'to keep her bit gear togither,' for which she was no more to be blamed than a dormouse abused for laziness because it sleeps out the winter. While taking refreshment at the hospitium of Skelwith Bridge having received pen, ink, paper, etc., from pretty Agnes, I wrote the following lines:

UPON my way I met a long, slow train
Of men and carts so silent that the rain
Through the still air distill'd, amid the hush
Was softly heard—more audible the gush
Of falling waters in their desperate leap,
And melancholy bleat of draggled sheep,
And moaning wheels—with solemn pace they trod
To lay beneath the church-yard's billowy sod
A woman, that had borne the woes and fears
And hopes of life—for nigh a hundred years;
That was a little Lassy in a frock
Ere the wild bird had planted in the rock
Yon tree—a wonder how its roots are fed
That decks the autumn with its beerries red.
She has outlived her loves. The world hath changed
Since she was young. The nimble feet that ranged
The lofty pastures—upward push'd the plough
Straight in the coffin they point upward now.
The oldest man that walks behind her hearse
Her middle age might see—a babe at nurse.[1]

---

[1] Published in Derwent Coleridge's *Memoir* of his brother, p. cxvi.

XIX

STILL is the morn—in peace the hamlet sleeps;
Soft—as the breath of sleep—the low mist sweeps
In gradual billows through the lowly dell;
But—hark—the sad, slow, intermittent knell,
That speaks of death—and halts—and speaks again—
As if it spake its last—and spake in pain—
Yet would—in every gasp of panting breath
Give breathing room for one good thought of death—
That doleful knell—tho' sad it sounds to thee—
Proclaims glad tidings of a victory—
A battle won—a warfare nobly ended—
Glad as the Trumpet tone that loud ascended
When Lucifer—with all his rebel host
O'erstep'd the last line of the heavenly coast
And Angels shouted to the Almighty throne—
Hosanna—Lord—for Heaven is all our own.
Yes—every boom of that dull swinging bell
Proclaims a victory—but who can tell
Who won the fight—and who has fought so well?
It was a Man—that long hath till'd a field
That only few—tho' precious fruits—can yield,
A minister of God—whose lengthened days
Were still increasing arguments of praise,
Who conn'd below—what he shall sing above,
The love of duty, and the song of love.
Though his the hardest task that God can give,
Yet he for God—was ever glad to live,
And though God gave him many an earthly tie
Of Love and Hope—he was full glad to die.
Content to live—while God had ought to do—
Complete his task—to God his spirit flew—
For many a year—and many here have known—
And some proclaim before the sacred throne,
From week to week he urged the gospel Truth,
Still to the young he pressed the perilous youth—
To middle age—the danger of much care—
And bid the old to make the most of prayer—
Though in his calling awful and severe,
So kind he was, his brow was still so clear—
Though faults he must have had—as Adam's Son—
Most were content to think that he had none,

Since not for might—but sanctity revered
In him—the holiest virtue was not feared—
To him had Nature given what man admires—
Sense, talent, eloquence, poetic fire,—
And studious labour had those gifts perfected,
With knowledge, which even sceptic wit respected,
But most his life, with every virtue fraught,
Enforced the lesson which his doctrine taught.
Full of good works he was—as full of days,
Long as he trod the world's mysterious maze;
Few years were wanting to his pilgrimage
To make his mortal life a secular age—
Yet—as in life beloved—beloved at last—
Who knew him—thought his life too short when past,
Now he receives the crown he well has earn'd—
And knows the Godhead he so long has learn'd.

XX

EPITAPH
ON AN HONEST HOSTESS

STRANGER, who e'er thou art, respect this stone.
The name it bears may be to thee unknown
And to the world. But it to *one* was dear
Or else it never had been sculptured here.
I will not ask thee for her soul to pray;
Pray for thy self, and all, and go thy way.

XXI

So Fare thee well—my little book—
Thou art a witness sad to me—
Of what a life, I once forsook—
To be—what least I thought to be.

I might have been—what hope and love
Would pray for whom they love the best—
And now I am—what God above
And only he can render blest.[1]

[1] This poem is at the end of one of Hartley Coleridge's notebooks; to it he prefixed the following note: 'And now am I arrived at the last page of this omnifarious miscellany—of prose, rhime, Greek, English, Criticism, and pure Nonsense. This little book was given me by one whom I cannot cease to love. . . . It was given me, just after I had made the important discovery that I could rhime—How I admired my own verses then—Here they are, sole written record of my happy years—

I know not whether I shall live to see my present works as old as these—or whether I shall esteem them as lightly—but sure I am I shall never love them so well. They are prophetic—the little piece called "Presentiment' [which appears on page 88] expressed the forebodings—which have been too fearfully fulfilled. I half regret that they may not repose alone unmixt, with the newer head-work of my latter day—But tattered as they are they shall have a secure asylum in my little box. . . . The days are now at the shortest—I hope that my days have been at the worst—There are some lines here of Ned Wilson's, one of the best of my College Chums, one I believe that really liked me—but I shall grow foolish—and it grows late———'

XXII

To love—and not be loved—is such my Fate?
Did God!—Oh! Could that gracious Sire create
A soul to feel and love his excellence
Yes—to adorn him with a faith intense
To love him in the earth and sky and sea,
Yet doom that soul to perish utterly?

XXIII

WITH much of fear, yet not without
Enough of hope to strive with doubt
I close December's eighteenth day.
What must I do? Fear—hope—and pray.[1]

December 18, 1841.

XXIV

"FOLLOWED BY ANOTHER[2]———

AH! woeful impotence of weak resolve,
Recorded rashly to the writer's shame,
Days pass away, and Time's large orbs revolve,
And every day beholds me still the same,
Till oft neglected purpose loses aim,
And hope becomes a flat unheeded lie,
And conscience weary with the work of blame,
In seeming slumber droops her wistful eye
As if she would resign her unregarded ministry.[3]

[*Nabbe, December,* 1848.]

---

[1] Published in *Hartley Coleridge: His Life and Work*, p. 156. Less than a month before his death Hartley Coleridge added this comment upon these lines: 'Alas—how true are these four lines—this present December 11—1848. How little progress have I made in this world—or towards Heaven.'

[2] 'A few months [or rather days] before his death, he [Hartley Coleridge] wrote the following affecting lines in a copy of his poems, alluding to his intention of publishing another Volume.' [Note by Derwent Coleridge.]

[3] Published in Derwent Coleridge's *Memoir* of his brother, p. clxxxviii.

XXV

PRESENTIMENT

SOMETHING has my heart to say
Something on my breast does weigh
That when I would full fain be gay
    Still pulls me back.

Something evil does this load
Most assuredly forebode,
So my experience sadly shew'd
    Too well I know.

Sometimes, as if with mocking guile
The pain departs a little while,
Then I can dance and sing and smile
    With merry glee—

But soon, too soon it comes again
The sulky, stifling, leaden pain,
As a black cloud is big with rain
    'Tis big with woe.

All I ask is but to know
The depth and nature of the woe.
I hope not for a wind to blow
    The cloud away.

I hear an inarticulate sound
Wherein no fixed sense is found
But sorrow, sorrow without bound
    Of what or where.[1]

[1] Published in Derwent Coleridge's *Memoir* of his brother, p. lxxxiii.

XXVI

TO AUGUSTA WITHINGTON

YEARS have past on and many a limber twig
Is grown a sapling Oak or taller pine
Since thou, Augusta, lived nigh Goody Brig
And wert a little merry pet of mine.
Now is thy toddle turned to movement staid
And thou, I hear, a grave and stately maid
Not all unconscious haply of the Name
Boasted of yore by Rome's imperial Dame—
But hard it is e'en for a man of Rhyme
To rule the working of the inward eye,
To make slow fancy vie with fleeting time
When time's becalmed on glassy memory.
I scarce can think so many days are past
That of so many friends I am the last,
Or that thy noble Father is laid low
Since thou werst Dusty and I Fal me ho—

alias Hartley Coleridge.

XXVII

TO THE OLD YEAR

FAREWELL—old comrade, thou wilt soon be dead,
Thy youthful honours long ago were shed,
And all the garlands of thy Summer pride—
And what thou hadst of Autumn—all have died,
And there is nothing more of thee to die
But half an hour of cold sterility.
Farewell—old Comrade—shall I call thee friend?
When thou wert born—I think I did intend
I hope I did not swear that I would mend—
Could I have known that the first new year's sun
Would rise upon me—and so little done—
Not any worthy work perform'd of mine
While thirty-eight has turned to thirty-nine
How much myself I had myself abhorr'd
Too like the thriftless servant of the Lord—
That thriftless servant of a Lord austere
That wrong'd his Lord from sloth and selfish fear.
And yet, old friend, since thou wilt soon be gone,
Friends let us part—the fount of Helicon
Has flow'd ere now upon a New Year's eve—
But now alas my brain is like the sieve
By those new-wedded virgins tended in the shades
That mock'd and marr'd the labour of the maids;
And yet one song I will for thee essay—
Ere that is sped, thou wilt be past away—
> Good Night—Good Night—Good Night to thee
> That with the Night must end,
> Old Year—I cannot say to thee—
> We'll meet again—old friend—
> For friend or foe—twixt thee and me
> No meeting evermore shall be.

XXVIII

Young friend, thou yet art young, and I
    Am growing very old,
And thou hast powers, which future hours
    Will perfect and unfold,
While I am waning to the west,
In truth, a great deal past my Best.

'Tis not my talent to advise
    Although my head is grey,
Old Time will never make me wise
    But thee, I hope, it may—
For that is in thee, I behold
That may be wise, when thou art old;

A strong intensity of Faith
    That can believe in good,
And Hope as strong, as wild bird's song
    Singing in native wood,
But most of all—sweet Charity—
That cast a friendly look on me.

XXIX

THE POET

Echo was erst a living nymph and warm,
With tears for woe, and sweet smiles to rejoice,
But hopeless love consumed her sentient form,
And nothing left her, but a helpless voice.
Much like a ghost, if old belief were true,
Which cannot speak, 'till it is spoken to—
And so the Poet, smit with love of fame,
Must vanish soon from this forgetful earth,
And be a nothing, save a voice, a name,
Which lives, when other voices give it birth,—
Yet, after death, what will it be to me
If a dead mark, or living echo be.[1]

[1] Published in *North of England Magazine*, February, 1842.

XXX

Nab—Dec. 18—1847.

DEAR SIR. My Surname Collridge isn't
I am a Coleridge Hartley christened.
The Bard—that did revisit Yarrow
Is smitten with a household sorrow;
His only daughter, dear beloved,
Is from this vale of tears removed.
And therefore you yourself must see
'Twould be an impropriety
For me or any other chap
To plague him for a single scrap—
Yet Joseph, if your name had been
Not Joseph, but sweet Josephine—
Fanny—or May—or simple Meg—
I might have been so bold to beg
For a few traces of his pen—
But autograph-collecting men
I know are his abominations
And so are all new corporations.
For—be't his weakness or his glory
He is a stubborn auld world Tory,
And would not choose his pen to stir
For Corporation officer
Tho'Joseph Dearden, 'tis by all allow'd,
Is one of whom proud Preston may be proud.[1]

---

[1] From an original manuscript in the possession of Professor H. W. Garrod. These lines were addressed by Hartley Coleridge to 'Mr. Joseph Dearden, Corporation Officer, Fishergate, Preston, Europe.'

XXXI
LINES——

I HAVE been cherish'd, and forgiven
  By many tender-hearted,
'Twas for the sake of one in Heaven
  Of *him* that is departed.

Because I bear my Father's name
  I am not quite despised,
My little legacy of fame
  I've not yet realized.

And yet if you should praise myself
  I'll tell you, I had rather
You'd give your love to me, poor elf,
  Your praise to my great father.

XXXII

Lack of matter, lack of brains,
Sore distracts the hapless swains
Who 'much metre, with much pains'
Endite for praise, or grosser gains
     Or smile of bonny Lasses—
Or to gain a lordly nod
Many for a rhyme will plod
And puzzle for a Heathen God
Or Hero, who beneath the sod
Has slumber'd many a period,
To whom they may compare my Lud,
     The pink of Maecen-Asses—

So Laureates—in ages back
For one poor annual butt of sack
Made Odes, which like the Almanack
Serv'd out their year, then served Pontac
     So soon their bays were blighted.
Such was the task of learned Ben,
So Daniel plied his sober pen,
And Davenant and eke Dryden,
Last of the race of noble Men,
Spake to the *venal* garland when
It crown'd Tom Shadwell, Tate, Eusden
     And Mister William Whitehead.

What though the courtly Laurel now
Adorn a true poetic brow;
Immortal Bard, as well might thou
Pay homage to a hugh Dutch Frau
     As big as all three Graces,
As well—nay better far—by half
Make Hymns to Jeroboam's Calf,
Or write in Sand an Epitaph
On the drown'd world of Mynheer Pfaff,
As waste thy precious autograph
Upon the mighty men of chaff
     That hit upon high places.

No doubt it is a noble thing
To be a harbinger of Spring
And year by year to tell the King
That every spray is blossoming
  A month before its Season,
That Phœbus has hold of his team
And heating with his native beam
The boiler, travels now by steam
To bless the land where reigns supreme
A monarch feted to redeem
The legal crown's primeval gleam
  And rule an age of Reason.

This were, indeed, a pleasant task
To ply, if annual butt and cask
Supplied the praise-inspiring flask,
Then Gaelick, Runic, Lettish, Basque,
  Norse, Coptic, Ethiopic,
Sanscrit, Pehlavee,[1] Hebrew, Perse,
Greek, Latin, Arabic, and Erse,
And infant Lingoes still at nurse
Spontaneous murmuring into verse,
As if relieved from Babel's curse,
Would blend their accents to disperse
  The song from Pole to Tropic.

How comes it, then, that all is still?
Dumb as in Gander's wing, the quill—
Glum! as the awkward squad at drill
The Bard presents no Hymn to Bill
  To George defunct, no Lament—
But true—the Laureate gets no sack—
Madeira—nor Frontignac—
Nor Sillery—nor yet Barsac—
Not e'en a noggin of Cognac,
And for the hundred pounds—alack—
He were a Fool indeed to rack
  His brain for such poor payment.

---

[1] Pahlavi.

XXXIII
FROM A LETTER TO MRS. GREEN

. . . You wish me to write a letter to enliven you—What liveliness can you expect from a solitary man in a small solitary room with no company but commonplace books—his own unfinished writings, a fireless grate, a wet miserable evening as my trowsers testify—and drinking of very small beer—all but myself in bed? Had you asked me for a lot of melancholy to dilute an excess of joyfulness I could have supplied you with a good Article—very cheap—but melancholy is a drug—not to be put off at any price—so I will try to be as lightsome as I can—The first topic which the English break out with is the weather—the next may be politicks or books—or their Neighbours—that last is—self— the sediment which lies at the bottom—whether it be weighty gold or thick and cumbrous—I will follow the national order— What weather we have—look out and about you—Green is the universal colour. . . .

You are asleep I trust, 'at this odd eve and dull watch of the night,' but I hear the wind not howling and whistling in November wise—but rushing and roaring and rumbling and tumbling

> Like a winter wind that had lost its way
> And in summer woods was far astray,
> From the shrill howling Desert a stranger arriving
> And a searcher that long in the sea hath been diving,
> And comes up with a weight of weed on his head
> Puffing like drowned man recalled from the dead,
> But climbing at last on a rock on the shore
> Looking around he gives a loud roar

Just as the wind is doing now—so enough about the weather— Now for Politicks and Neighbours. No doubt you have heard of Mr. Wordsworth's accession to the vacant laureateship—He is to hold it as a sinecure—I wish he would appoint me his Deputy—No Laureate ever attained the wreath under more propitious circumstances—The Queen was delivered of a Daughter—The Duke of Sussex died—He should have composed a pastoral dialogue of alternate lamentation and rejoicing—Damon and Strephon something in this way—

Strephon—Why Damon, why in sable suit to-day
When Joy should turn December into May?
Dost thou not hear how all the valleys sing
And the hoarse cataracts roar 'God save the King'?
The snowdrops dying wish to live a bit,
The birds of winter now are loth to flit,
The Daffodil impatient bursts its sheath,
The oak leaves earlier cut their scalloped teeth,
The Earth is glad—the Ocean rolls in glee
And all the Maids of Honour cry he, hee—
Methinks the world is drunk with laughing gas—
And why? Victoria has a little lass.

Damon— I had a tup, I had but one alack!
His horns were quaintly wreathed, his wool was
black,
But he is dead—the Duke is dead also,
And therefore do I wear this garb of woe—
Oh dear the tup is dead and Sussex too
And therefore I have spun my [*sic*]
The sable fleece has made my jerkin sable—
Strephon sit down and let's be miserable.

Strephon—Why that's a thing I never like at all;
Hang care, say I, let markets rise or fall,
Let Norfolk pine at too abundant crops,
Let Kent look glum with fear of failing hops,
But as for me—I'll never pipe my eye
For Queens can breed as fast as Dukes can die.

XXXIV
PARODY ON WORDSWORTH

HE lived amidst th' untrodden ways
  To Rydal Lake that lead:—
A bard whom there were none to praise,
  And very few to read.

Behind a cloud his mystic sense,
  Deep-hidden, who can spy?
Bright as the night, when not a star
  Is shining in the sky.

Unread his works—his 'Milk-white Doe'
  With dust is dark and dim;
It's still in Longman's shop, and Oh!
  The difference to him![1]

---

[1] Published in *Notes and Queries*, June 19, 1869. Hartley Coleridge's authorship
of this poem established loc cit., July 24, 1869.

XXXV
PETER BELL

A satire upon the Poet Laureate's celebrated production.[1]

COME listen, my friend, Stephen Otter,
  Pope and Dryden I mean to surpass
With a tale of a wonderful potter
  And a very remarkable Ass.

For the potter his name it was Peter,
  Sure some of you know Peter Bell,
But as for the Donkey poor *creatur*
  What they called it I never could tell.

Some poets begin in the middle
  And some by invoking a muse,
But that's only like tuning the fiddle
  And in fact not of half so much use.

But you like to hear the beginning,
  Of a Life all the ins and the outs,
And to go as far back as the pinning
  Of the hero in swaddling clouts.

[1] Hartley Coleridge never wrote down this parody, but Joseph Burns, one of his friends, made a transcript. After Hartley's death Burns threatened to publish these lines, as well as others of somewhat the same nature. Derwent and Sara Coleridge were greatly alarmed. ' A *jeu d'esprit*,' Derwent wrote to Burns of this parody, 'which however harmless when recited in the *safe* retirement of a domestic circle for the amusement of his friends, no real friend of my Brother would for obvious reasons permit to see the light.' Burns by no means agreed. 'There is also,' he wrote, 'a Ballad of Peter Bell, a severe satire on Wordsworth's *precious effusion* under the same name, which was never committed to paper by my friend, fearful it should meet the eye of some mutual acquaintance. I prevailed on him however not long ago to repeat it slowly so that I might transcribe it to paper, under a promise it should never be made use of during his life time—unfortunately it is only a fragment, but of such a nature that I feel confident it would soon rivet the attention of Men of letters——' Burns was, however, prevented from publishing this poem, and it is printed here for the first time.

An amusing sidelight on Wordsworth's own *Peter Bell* is found in Burns's unpublished memoir of Hartley Coleridge: 'In 1815 Mr. Wordsworth accompanied young Coleridge to Merton College, Oxford, for the purpose of facilitating his studies, and introducing him to some friends. On arriving at Woodstock they discovered that a Trunk had been stolen at Stratford-upon-Avon, containing some of Coleridge's apparel—a pelisse of Mrs. Wordsworth's as well as the manuscript of Peter Bell, a ballad composed some time previous, but not published till five years afterwards. The Trunk and Manuscript were afterwards found on a Dunghill! The event very much disconcerted Mr. W. who attributed more value to Peter Bell than to Mrs. W.'s satin mantle.'

Of ancestry lineage and such like
  Their lengthy narration to swell
Is a thing that Welch bards very much like—
  Of what family came Peter Bell?

If his linaege was Saxon or Norman
  Or Danish no annals record,
His father might perhaps be a Carman
  He *possibly* might be a Lord.

A MOTHER most certainly had he,
  An itinerant dealer in delf,
But she ne'er told him who was his daddie,
  For she wasn't quite certain herself.

Howso'er his existence began near
  A Hayrick, for there he was whelp'd;
His cradle was nought but a pannier—
  'Tis low but it cannot be help'd.

You have heard of those wonderful Minors
  That were nursed by a Wolf, I dare say;
So had Peter an ass for his drynurse,
  And she lull'd him to sleep with her bray.

Dame Nature will sometimes exhibit
  Prophetical marks in the skin,
So Peter was mark'd with a gibbet,
  The sign of original sin.

For Peter no mortal was sponsor,
  For he never was christened, poor lamb;
So *God-mother* sure he had none, Sir,
  Yet the first word he lisp'd was *god dam.*

Than Peter no lad cut be 'cuter
  Yet he often had wanted a meal,
If the Tinker his travelling Tutor
  Had not trained his young genius to steal.

XXXVI

Wordsworth, being born at Cockermouth might be styled the Gander of Cocker, as Shakespeare was termed the Swan of Avon.

WHEN we are dead and gone to Davy's Locker,
Still shall thy name survive, great Goose of Cocker.

XXXVII

[In a letter to Mary Claude, Hartley Coleridge remarked: 'For the benefit . . . of her [Mrs. H. M. Rathbone, editor of *Childhood*, 1841] more juvenile readers she is welcome to the following ditty, which though simple I really think has much natural passion. But you must not let the mercantile or dissenting public conceive that it is ascribed to the Bard of Rydal Mount. . . . Reflecting that Mrs. Rathbone is a member of the Society of Friends, I am apprehensive that the Exclamation—My eye—may appear too like an oath. She will use her own enlightened judgement.']

LOLLY-POPS
And nice mint drops
They are my dear delight;
For Sugar Candy
I'm the Dandy—
Be it brown or white.
A toffy stick
Will make me lick
Like any cur—my chops—
On Ginger-bread
I would be fed
And dainty sugar-sops.
And Figs and Prunes
And Macaroons
And Oranges also—
And raisins dry
And Plums. My eye
But they are all the go.

[*Knabbe, November* 18, 1840.]

XXXVIII

BUTTER'S ETYMOLOGICAL SPELLING BOOK, &c.

BUTTER's books I ne'er have read,
I hope they butter him his bread,
But such is Youth's depravity
And so averse to gravity,
They'd rather dabble in the gutter
Than learn to spell of Mr. Butter;
Yes their perverseness is so utter
They'd rather eat than study butter.

XXXIX

ON A DISSOLUTION OF MINISTRY

SHOUT Britain, raise a joyful shout,
The Tyrant Tories all are out—
Deluded Britons—cease your din—
For lo—the scoundrel Whigs are in.

XL

I DREAMED that buried in my fellow clay
Close by a common beggar's side I lay,
And as so mean an object shock'd my pride,
Thus like a corpse of consequence I cry'd,
'Scoundrel, begone, and henceforth touch me not,
More manners learn and at a distance rot.'
'How! scoundrel!' with a hautier tone cry'd he,
'Proud lump of earth, I scorn thy words and thee,
Here all are equal, now thy case is mine,
This is my rotting place, and that is thine'.

XLI

REASONS FOR NOT WRITING IN DECEMBER 1842

THE sadden'd year has but few days to live
And now seems mourning for its own decay,
What merry rhyme should a poor Poet give
Fit for a maid so innocent and gay.

When winter glitters all with sunny frost
And chrystal gems are hung on every branch
And morning blades with powdery rime embost
Crisply beneath light footsteps crackling cranch;

When streets and roads ring sharp below the wheel
And the flat lake appears a marble floor
And shooting—arrow swift on shoes of steel
The skaters wake blithe echo from the shore;

Then may a bard, though haply stiff and old,
Earn with a jocund verse a lassy's kiss—
But what can I do that have got a cold
On such a muggy, mizzling morn as this?

XLII

A CALM HOUR IN A CHURCHYARD

WE sat—our comrades were the sleeping dead—
So solemn and so calm the autumn sky,
So very calm appear'd the lowly bed,
Methought it were a blessed thing to die.

Smooth was the lake—so willing to reflect
The pensive silence of the brooding Heaven—
It seemed an image of the retrospect,
The mute communion of the blest eleven*—

With such a silence as the watchful clouds—
E'en now have kept—and with a peace as still
As those that lie about us in their shrouds—
Nor heave—nor pant—each in their own green hill—

Oh—in such stillness could we keep our mind
That it might still reflect the Lord on High—
We need not care for hail or rain or wind,
For then we always should be fit to die.

---

*Long had they prayed—and much no doubt had talk'd—
For very much they must have had to tell;
And here they parted—It was no ghost that walk'd
But their own Jesus whom they loved so well—

XLIII

THE OLD CHURCH'S LAMENT

LIKE to a time-worn bark, wrecked on some rock-bound strand,
Thus lonely and deserted on the steep hill's side I stand
Quiet and silent, guarding with pious care the consecrated
    ground,
And shadowing still with sacred power the holy graves around.
Oh! give me yet one gentle thought, ye hasty passers-by,
Oh! give me for my pleasant memories but one gentle sigh.
Ah! 'midst the noise and bustle of this busy life,
With all its daily ceaseless toil and strife,
Like yon sweet river's murmuring voice that sounds
From the green vale through which it speeds and quickly bounds,
And as it glides along still soothes the listening ear
As if some heavenly music sounded near,
So shall my memories call up many a train
Of bygone happy visions, thought on not in vain.

XLIV

TO LITTLE ANNIE GIBSON

WOULD I were good enough to bless
Thee Child, so early motherless,
So lovely, to provoke caress
    And childlike words
And murmuring sounds, as meaningless
    As song of Birds.

To see thee tripping on the way
And lifting up thy face so gay
Like glow-worm in thy black array
    And tidy bonnet
'Twould move the hardest heart to say
    'God's blessing on it.'

If Innocence were like the measles,
If pure thoughts stuck to us like teazles
And were not like the seeds of thistles
    So light and flimsy
Borne off by every wind that whistles
    To every whimsy—

Could I remain—what holding thee
My little maiden, on my knee—
E'en to myself I seem to be,
    Then like a Seer—
With voice and power of prophesy
    I'd bless thee dear.

XLV

THERE was a cot, a little rustic home,
Which oft I used to pass in careless youth,
Where a sweet child was growing like a flower
In the high fissure of a mossy crag,
Giving a kind and human loveliness
To bleakest soltiude—I know not why
In all my rambles, still my steps were led
To that lone dwelling,—still—if e'er I missed
The little maiden with her sun-burn'd face,
Her rosy face that glowed with summer brown,
Quick glancing through the lattice, my heart sank
And all that day my thoughts were matterless
As if defrauded of their daily bread;
But when she lilted from the lowly door
Tossing her burden of crisp, curly locks
That kept her arms in pretty motion still
To give free prospect to her wild blue eyes,
My soul was glad within me, as the deep
Glows with the young light of the sudden Sun,
For three long years I watch'd her, and she seem'd
To greet my coming as a natural thing,
The punctual quitrent of unfailing time.

XLVI

LINES

DEAR little maid, I dare not love thee more
Because I know, I still must love in vain;
Thy love of one, whose head is early hoar
To him no hope affords, to thee, no stain.

That I have loved thee, cannot be thy boast
When thy young beauties bloom in summer's glory,
Nor will I come, an uninvited Ghost,
To tell thee, all thy charms are transitory.

To love thee and to know how sweet and fair
Thou art, is recompense enough for me,
'Tis all I ought to ask or wish to share
With him whom God hath destined worthy thee.

XLVII

TO JAMES, SON OF T. JACKSON, ON HIS
FOURTH BIRTHDAY

Four years—a very little time they seem,
To childhood longer is an half hour's dream,
Yet 'tis to thee thy total sum of Being
Thine all of breathing, feeling, stirring, seeing.
Little thou knowst of sorrow—Boy—as yet,
Or sorrow which a moment may forget—
The nearest woe to thee was like an arrow
Which only missed thee by a space so narrow
No term of measure fitly can express
Its infinitely little Littleness.
But 'tis most true, as one great poet saith,
'A little child—what can it know of death?'
No more—than any can conceive of birth—
Darkness abides upon the ends of earth
And all the world in which we live and see
Rolls in a deep abyss of mystery.
The light that makes all beauty and discloses
Fair Girls, and placid Lakes, and opening Roses
Comes from a source afar, through boundless dark!
Beyond the highest pitch of morning lark,
Is a vast gulf of darkness and of cold—
All lifeless, objectless, forlornly old—
The light—it is not light—till something meets
That gives existence to the light it greets—
And even so—is man ordained to be.
No more is told to wise men than to thee—
My little Lad—of four long happy years
Of gushing laughter and of transient tears.
May God vouchsafe thee just enough of light
From day to day to guide thy steps aright.

XLVIII

TO DR. BRIGGS, ON HIS 70TH BIRTH-DAY

'Three score and ten I can remember well.'
SHAKESPEARE

'THREE score and ten I can remember well',—
  Happy the man that having liv'd so long
  Still finds within himself the purpose strong
To live, as he has liv'd, and still live well.

Three score and ten, so holy dirges tell,
  Is the last bourne of happy human life;
  Yet with the best of youthful feelings rife
Thy soul lives still, because thou hast liv'd well.

If cavern'd close, in hermit's rocky cell
  In wilful ignorance of all the world,
  Like blighted bud, within itself upcurl'd,
To thine own self to live, and so live well.

If such had been thy choice, alone to dwell,
  Lone as the flow'ret on the pathless wild—
  Sworn to thyself, for aye to be a child,
No wonder then, that thou hadst liv'd so well.

But thou wert no such piping Philomel,
  To wail in darkling copse ideal sorrow,
  'Twas still thy thought at night, how on the morrow
So to live on, that others might live well.

Each hour to thee, repeating its own knell,
  Still spake of duty done, or yet to do,
  For soul or body, for the twain, if two
One duty are, for him that would live well.

And so good memories are a holy spell
  To aid thy weakness and to calm thy pains,
  And thou art happy that the thought remains
That thou hast liv'd so long, and liv'd so well.

XLIX

SWEET I saw you—coyly sitting,
Every feature well-befitting,
Dress in every point adjusted,
Far too nicely to be trusted
From the side of that old woman—
But there came a youth to summon
You to join him in quadrilling
And oh! I thought—you were but too, too willing.
    I sat in a corner
    Like little Jack Horner,
    Curled up like a Cat
    When she smells a big Rat.
    I saw you advancing
    On tiptoe for dancing;
    Like a Statue from Greece
    All still in your beauty
    You stood—every crease
    Of your robe did its duty.
    Your Swain look'd contented
    At his pumps so well black'd,
    While I was demented
    And sorely tormented
    As Heretic rack'd;
    I thought his silk stocking
    My pain was a-mocking.
Methought I could have stung him like a snake
But no—my Love—I loved him for your sake.

Sweetly smiling—you stood still—
But lo—the music loud and shrill
Sets the dancers all a-stirring—
There must be an end of purring
    Now you meet
    Now retreat
Now another's place you gain,
Glancing backward at your swain,
Now you are at home again
And sweetly pant behind your fan
As Syrinx when she fled from Pan.

Like a new thought in Poet's brain
The music now breaks forth again—
I see the curious lines ye trace
Fine as the patterns of old lace—
Fain would I tame my quaking heart
To think it all a work of art,
Like mad dance of extatic Bacchanals
Reveal'd afresh on Herculaneum Walls.
But hark the music ceases—I am left
Alone amid the crowd, even of my dream bereft—
Now round the gay saloon in stately walk,
Pace the gay couples, linked in earnest talk.

L

It is the merry month of May—
The flowers have come in troops,
With yellow green, the old oak is gay—
And the grey-green willow droops;
The Year is young as it was of yore
But woe—and alas—we are young no more.

'Twas on the merry first of May—
'Tis very long since then,
Great George the third then held the sway
O'er noble Englishmen—
The Cat beside the fire was purring—
Your spinning wheel was whirring, whirring,
I said—this is no day to spin
Come out and dance with me—
You said—ah, no 'twould be a sin
For my little brothers three
And my Father also are sick in their bed
And only last year, my mother was dead.
I stood—I could not get away—
Your wheel was turning still,
You minded not, what I could say,
But with a constant will
You counted your threads and span and span
As if there were no such thing as a man;
At last you lifted up your head,
'Twas in your quiet way,
But oh! with what a look you said
You're wanted at the May.

I looked at you once—and I bade Goodbye—
I went a few steps—and I heard a sigh.

I stopt awhile—I felt a thrill
Oh Lord if it should be;
I paused again, and I heard a sob
It could not be for me.
There was noise far away—but all was still
No sound was nigh but the tinkling rill.

It was the merry month of May
And the Cuckoo shouted strong,
I really did not know my way
Or how to get along—
And so I went back and I saw you at rest
In thought crooking down—with your arms on your breast.

It is the merry month of May
Then you were young—and so was I—
Then let us good old folks be gay
Nor what we said before deny.

'Twas Spring, my Love, when first we met
As you may well remember—
That meeting we do not regret
Though now it is December—
Oh! Dame of my love—with thy locks of grey
Thou art lovely to me as the Lady of May.

LI

Written in a Copy of Sara Coleridge's *Phantasmion*

SHE that once was like a Fairy—
Just as light, and just as airy,
Whose every word was like a spell,
Sounded on a pearly shell—
Or harp—which wandering bard and blind
Has left to prattle with the wind—
When a suffering Matron, tried—
By grief—subdued and mortified
In pious woe—her God adoring
And thankful most, when most imploring—
Recalling images and sounds
That model'd once the frolic bounds
And glancing movements of the child
To soothe and lull the Matron mild—
Composed this tale—this waking dream
This murmur of a distant stream—
This shadow of a purple mist
Of self-diffusing Amethyst—
If one heart—it may disburthen
Of a weary bond of pain—
Then my Sister—lovely northen—
Has not lived or wrote in vain.[1]

---

[1] From an original manuscript in the possession of the Armitt Library, Ambleside.

LII

TO THE RIVER OTTER IN DEVONSHIRE

OTTER, what boots it, say, that through the vale
With dull, inglorious wave you rolled along?
What boots it, that unnoticed in the dale
Till now you never waked the muse's song?
The time is come, when brightening in to day
Far above prouder streams thy name shall soar
And endless flourish, in the Poet's lay,
When even in memory Thames shall be no more.
For lo! beneath a neighbouring roof of late
Fast by thy willowy side a bard was born:
August in strains majestically great
Or light as carols of the bird of morn,
Whose vivid lines in glowing colours clad,
Bid indignation raise an angry cry
Or dulcet notes with variation sad,
Call forth the ready tear from Pity's streaming eye.
Sweet River! see thy favoured banks along
Flashes with orient rays the western star:
Sweet River! flow thy envied meads among
For thou and Coleridge are a deathless pair.

LIII

ON A PICTURE REPRESENTING GYPSIES
AND ASSES

GYPSIES and Asses. Subjects of all weather!
No doubt the Artist found you both together.
Alike you live from law and tax exempt,
Alike the objects of the world's contempt;
And yet the mother's instinct strong in each
The selfsame lesson seems in both to preach,
That the same nature, the same law sublime,
Prevails in every kind in every clime.
In Ass and Gypsy—both alike we trace
An antique pedigree, an eastern race,
Perhaps the Babe that on that woman's shoulder
Now looks so old, it hardly can grow older—
Sprung from a mother Queen—it may be one
Of the seven hundred wives of Solomon—
Perhaps the Ass that with a look so mild
And languid hangs upon her hapless child,
Is born of one by Israel's brood bestrid
Beneath the shade of new rais'd pyramid,
That trode the bottom of the subject water,
Proud of the weight of Israel's fairest daughter,
When Moses ruled the Red Sea with his rod,
And ocean's self did homage to its God,
Perhaps, poor Ass, thy sire, if not thy dam
Crouch'd to the stroke of greedy Balaam.
Or it may be, indeed we cannot tell,
Of that white band that trotted blithe and well
Ruined by a son of the Judge of Israel.
Poor thing, methinks that in thy face I see
A cast of oriental dignity,
A desperate patience, that would fain impart
The lessons of an o'er experienced heart
To that dear shaggy infant at thy side,
That dreams not *yet* of what it must abide.

LIV

On the Death of Echo, a favourite Beagle belonging to the late Robert
Partridge, Esq., and engraved on a stone Tablet placed over the spot where
it was buried in the field behind Covey Cottage——

SILENT at last, beneath the silent ground
Here Echo lives, no unsubstantial sound
Nor babbling mimic—but a Beagle fleet
With drooping ears, keen nose, and nimble feet.
In the glad Chase she raised her merry voice
And made her name-sake of the woods rejoice,
But now dumb Death has choked poor Echo's cry
And to no call can Echo more reply—

LV

'TIS howling night—good men and happy sleep,
Or if awake—they watch the pattering rain,
They whisper one short prayer, and sleep again.
Some sickly babe mayhap awakes to weep—
For baby fear or sharp short fit of pain;
The hind dim dozing—dreams about his sheep
Or cattle, pelted in the plashy plain.
But hark! the loud wind comes—with perilous sweep
Down the straight valley. Woe for them that roam
Abroad this night. If some forgotten shed
Or smoke-stain'd ruin that was once a home
Yield a damp pillow to the vagrant head,
There let them slumber till the cocks a-crowing
Tell the poor Ghosts, they better had be going.

But what do I—at such a time of night
Of such a night when the swift scudding moon
Like hunted hart—pursued by many a loon
Through glancing thicket—and unwelcome light
Thrids the dark scattered clouds in anxious flight;
What makes me a mute listener to the roar
That rattles on the casement, shakes the door
Enough to rouse a praying Anchorite?

LVI

IT comes—it goes—it ebbs—it flows—
It comes again—and no one knows—
How much of good it hath been doing
Or half its work of woe—and ruin—
It comes with a sweep and a curl, and a swell,
As if it had some thing mighty to tell,
And it steals away—when its tale is told—
Like a thing that was chidden for being too bold—
But yet it has been, we cannot tell where—
It hath been where the bold ship never dare—
Come near, where the howling sea-dogs bark
Ever and aye in the cavern'd dark—
It hath winded along the crankling creeks
To meet the small rivulets, silvery streaks,
That gave light to the inbound green and brown—
It hath wash'd the cities of high renown—
And the castles—the antique walls that frown
On the thoughtless course of the tripping tide
That used to reflect them in all their pride.[1]

---

[1] This poem is contained in a letter, in which Hartley Coleridge wrote: 'I do not know the particular aspect of the shore or the Sea that compose your present prospect—I never saw the Sea without a sense of glory—which I can—perhaps—better express in verse than prose— . . . [These are] very bad verses truly. But if you had been with me on the coast of the Isle of Wight where the woods come down to high-water mark—(Heaven preserve them from the ax, I speak of twenty years ago) and there [letter breaks off thus.]

LVII

REMEMBRANCE OF GENOA

I AM where snowy mountains round me shine
    But in sweet vision truer than mine eyes,
    I see pale Genoa's marble crescent rise
Between the water and the Apennine.

On the sea-bank she couches like a Deer,
    A creature giving light with her soft sheen,
    While the blue ocean, and the mountain green
Pleased with the wonder always gaze on her.

And day and night the mild sea-murmur fills
    The corridors of her cool palaces,
    Carrying the freshness from the orange trees
A fragrant gift unto the peaceful hills.

And from the balustrades into the street
    From time to time there are voluptuous showers,
    Gentle descents of shaken lemon flowers
Stirr'd by the echo of the passing feet.

And when the sun his noon day height hath gain'd
    How mute is all that slumberous Appennine
    Upon whose base the streaks of green turf shine
With the black olive gardens interveined.

How fair it is when in the purple bay
    Of the soft-sea the clear-edged moon is drinking
    Or the dark-sky amid the ship-masts winking
With summer lightning over Corsica.

O Genoa—thou art a marvellous birth,
    A clasp which joins the mountains and the sea,
    And the two powers do homage unto thee
As to a matchless wonder of the earth.

Can life be common life in spots like these—
    Where they breathe breath from orange gardens wafted?
    Thy joy and sorrow surely must be grafted
On stems apart for these bright Genoese!

LVIII

LAUGH NO MORE

A BALLAD IN BEHALF OF POOR PADDY.

SACRA RES MISER EST.

The Profits to be given to the Irish Relief Fund

Poor Paddy has served for a joke very long,
His bulls and his brogue make a right merry song,
And we lik'd him the better the more that we laugh'd
At the praties he eat, the poteen that he quaff'd.

But Paddy in misery, gnawing a bone,
Is no longer the Paddy that once cried Och-hone!
When his children are hungry his heart must be sore,
Oh then, my good fellows, laugh at him no more.

Of Norah 'twas once very pleasant to talk,
But her lily white skin is now paler than chalk,
And dim are the eyes, and the hands long and lean
Of the erewhile bright-eyed and white-handed Kathleen.

He that wielded shelalagh at Donnybrook fair,
Now sits by the road-side in famish'd despair;
He will eagerly mumble the morsel you give,
But he knows not and cares not how long he may live.

But let not the weight of the want and distress
Make *our* love grow cold or our charity less;
Let those who have little give all that they can,
Let them give for one day but a meal to one man.

Believe, that the Maker of Heaven and Earth
Has for merciful purpose appointed this dearth,
That Irish and English may feel for each other,
As men ought to feel who are sons of one mother.

The seasons will mend, and the cool breath of morn
And soft dews of evening will foster the corn,
And potatoes will grow undiseased on the plain,
And then we may laugh at poor Paddy again.[1]

[Price threepence.]

[1] From a printed copy in the possession of Merton College, Oxford. Hartley Coleridge was greatly concerned over the Irish Famine and wrote several poems, which were printed and sold, as his contribution to the Irish Relief Fund.

LIX

TRANSLATION FROM THE GERMAN

HEART of mine, what art thou ailing?
What means thine Oh! and well a day?
Art not thou well—with strangers dwelling?
What wantst thou more, dear Heart, Oh say?[1]

What do I want? All things and ever
I want—so much forlorn I be—
Fair is the stranger land, but never
Can this land be a home to me.

There's no one here to love us dearly,
No one so warm to press the hand,
No not a babe to smile so cheerly
As at our home in Switzerland.[2]

[1] The following stanza represents Hartley Coleridge's second attempt to translate the first stanza from the German:

Heart of mine—what art thou ailing?
What means thine alack—and woe is me?
Have we not here a good fair dwelling?
What dost thou want in a strange countrie?

[2] Hartley Coleridge translated from the following stanzas, which are adapted from the Swiss poem of Joh. Rudolf Wyss der jüngere (1781–1830).

Herz mein Herz warum so traurig
Und was soll das Ach und Weh!
's Ist ja schön im fremden Lande,
Herz mein Herz was fehlt dir mehr?

Was mir fehlt? mir fehlt ja alles,
Bin so ganz verlassen hier.
Zwar is schön im fremden Lande
Doch zur Heimath wird es nie.

Keiner hat was lieb da draussen
Keiner drückt so warm die Hand
Und kein Kindlein will mehr lächeln
Wie daheim im Schweizerland.

LX

TRANSLATION FROM THE FRENCH[1]

'CELESTIAL BUTTERFLY,' thus spake the flower, with sighs,
    "Thou soar'st away,
While I—alas!—so different are our destinies,
    Perforce must stay!

'Yet we do love, and far from haunts of men we live
    In sunny bowers;
We are so much alike, one name to both they give—
    Two kinds of flowers.

'When high in air, upborne on pinions broad and light
    Thou dost recline,
Ah! then t' embalm with choicest scent thy hovering flight,
    Earth-chained I pine!

'It may not be! thou fliest too far, all flow'rets sweet
    Thou 'rt free to range;
But I must stay alone and watch, while at my feet
    The shadows change.

'Thou fliest to and fro, and each new spot thy grace
    Adorns and cheers:
While still the early morning finds my pensive face
    Wet, with cold tears.

"Oh! that our love in equal stream flow evermore,
    E'en as it springs—
Like me, do thou take root, or that I skyward soar,
    Give me thy wings.'

    L'Envoy to——
Oh, rose and butterfly, the grave unites at last
    Or late or soon;
Say will ye wait, or live together ere is past
    The summer noon?

[1] These lines, including L'Envoi à . . ., are freely translated from Victor Hugo's poem, *La Pauvre Fleur disait au Papillon.* (See *Les Chants du Créspuscule.*)

Somewhere above in heaven if thou those regions fair
    Dost yearn to measure—
Or somewhere in the field, if thy sweet chalice there
    Pours forth its treasure,

Where'er thou wilt, it matters not, if breath thou art
    Or colour's flame—
If wing of radiant butterfly or flow'ret's heart—
    They are the same.

To be together still, at morn, at noon, at even—
    That is our need!
Then we may choose by chance, or earth or heaven,
    Nor greatly heed!

LXI

ADA OF GRASMERE

In Grasmere's woods is a crystal well
In the very heart of a shadowy dell;
The sparkling beck leaps merrily down
Over fissure and chasm and crag,
Never a moment its waters lag,
Streaming from the sunny crown
Of that green hill, steep and high—
Never a moment its ripples die
Till it lies in still delight,
Beautiful and calm and bright,
In its rocky basin of chrysolite.

Ada of the flaxen hair
And eyes as blue as the heaven's sheen,
Sat in dreamy musing there,
And watched the glassy bubbles rise,
Till the waters cool and green
Mocked her with strange effigies,
And she saw in the mystic hyaline
By the light of a single star,
One who in alien lands afar
Fought for holy Palestine—
And there came—O strange and weird!
Rising faerily, whispering aerily,
A soft voice from the placid spring,
And sorrowful eyes of lustre peered
Through the aspen boughs above her,
And it seemed as if a fluttering wing
Of spirit addrest to some wondrous quest
Waved the holy fountain over.

—Ada of Grasmere! If they be
True vows that thou hast pledged to me,
Me, thine own Lord Florian,
When the midnight glories rise
Come thou out beneath the skies!
At the last sound of the midnight bell
From thy fragrant couch arise,

And braid a lily in thy hair,
And that single ruby wear
Around thy slender finger white,
I gave thee on that saddest night
When last I press'd thy lips divine,
Beside the waters of this well,
Ere I went, a sworded man,
To the holy cities of Palestine—

—'O Florian! My Florian!'
Thus the Lady Ada cried,
'Is it, is it truly thou?
Or some fierce unhallowed sprite
Troubling my vision of delight!
Saint Sybilla! aid me now!'
She knelt beneath the beechen bough
Heavy with its summer leaves,
And gazed into the heavens wide,
And with prayer was sanctified.

O holy prayer! The heart that grieves
Under the shadow of deep distress—
Death, or peril, or human wrong—
Using thee in humbleness,
Shall be at peace.

Those elms among,
Beautiful Ada softly prayed,
Nor any longer was afraid,
But stood beneath the starry cope
All joy, and loveliness, and hope,
And wrapt her in her vesture white.
Thus past in beauty through the night,
Once glancing at the mystic well.
And again these accents fell
On the lady's listening ear,
Heard with more of love than fear—
'In the lonely midnight be thou here!'

The Lady Ada onward went
Through the woods to her father's
        hall;
A thousand sounds aerial

Floated around her on her way.
It was that solemn hour of day
When the great emblazonment
Of the sunset dies away,
When very tranquil, very calm,
In the whole region of the sky,
And he whom it delights to lie
Listening to the sound of waters
Dreams of the blue Heaven's fabled
    daughters,
And drinks the music of a psalm
Which his wandering fancy brings
Down to earth on its waving wings.

Onward the Lady Ada past,
And softly to her chamber crept,
And knelt beside her couch and wept,
Wept wildly forth a sorrowful prayer
(Which the Spirit of Mercy answered
    there),
And on her yielding bed she cast
Her lovely form, and slept.
—'Lady Ada! now awake
For thine own Lord Florian's sake!'
Thus a voice of vision chanted,
As came on the lonely hour;
And Ada struggled, and sighed, and
    panted
In her sleep, as one enchanted,
Wrestling with unearthly power;
But the voice so pure and faint
Louder[1] raised the song of plaint,
    And ever said
'Lady Ada! now awake
For thine own Lord Florian's sake!'

Ada arose, most beautiful,
Threw off her silken coverlet
Which her snowy breast had kissen,
And thoughts most strange began to glisten
In her large eyes of violet;
Then, of timorous gladness full,
She robed her in her raiment white,

[1] Dander *in printed copy.*

White as the single lily flower
Braided in her flaxen hair,
And veiled from the voluptuous sight
Of stray spirits of the night,
The loveliness which was her dower.

Whispering a quiet prayer,
Ada threw wide her chamber door
And softly trod the creaking floor,
Gliding on her shadowy way
Like some silver-footed fay.
The galleries were long and dim,
Long and dim, with rushes strewn;
Through painted forms of seraphim,
Shone the faint sweet summer moon.
All without was dense and green,
A mavis scarce could glide between
The thick leaves 'tween the oriels high,
That opened proudly to the sky.
Into the court-yard past she forth—
All was still and silent there,
And soon she trod the warm green earth,
Where the great boughs swung to an eerie tune
Under the eye of the tranquil moon,
And to herself with moving lip
Whispered still a quiet prayer;
For she heard in all that stirred—
Footstep of the startled fawn
Pattering o'er the even lawn—
Old grey mossy fountain's drip—
In ought that stirred sweet Ada heard
That wondrous voice of hope and fear,
—'In the lonely midnight be thou here!'

Ada of the flaxen hair
And eyes as blue as the summer sea
Stood at length in silence there,
By the magic fountain's brink,
Where oft the red deer pause to drink,
And, mirrored in the ripples free,
Very clear could Ada see
The fragile lily in her hair,
And on her finger the ruby bright
That seemed to startle the silver night.

This was the Lady Ada's cry,
—'Holy One! who cannot die,
Camest, yea, to die for me
Who hath despite done to Thee,—
And did'st feel the proud man's scorn
And the woe of one forlorn,—
Whose heavenly eyes did brim with
    tears
For the sorrows of human years—
Whose holy hands were pierced through,
Whose feet long toil and travel knew,
Who felt all grief, all wild despair
That the race of men may ever bear,—
O look down from thy placid sky
Upon a maiden worn with woe,
Who in her snowy chastity
Hast past the years of life below!—
O let no spirit of affright
Visit me this ghastly night!'

So she prayed; and listening
Stood beside the magic spring,
But only heard the brooklet's splash,
And the berries fall from the mountain
    ash,
And the cry of birds in the woods away,
And the step of the roe o'er the lichens
    grey.

Yet at length—ah, who shall tell
In the lonely midnight what befell?
Whether on a spirit steed
Came the noble Florian,
And bore away with tempest speed
Ada of the flaxen hair,
Before the tremulous stars began
To fade into the daylight air;
Or if into the fairy chasm
Rent by mighty earthquake's spasm
The two lovers suddenly sank
From the mountain's mossy bank,
Who can tell? We may not tell
In that weird midnight what befell.

Lord Delaval of Grasmere Hall
With a hundred vassals rode
Wakening the woods to his trumpet-call,
And sent a thousand troopers forth
Over the borders of the north:
And northward went the stalwart band,
Spur on heel, and lance in hand,
And dashed along the echoing road,
And every border Castle bade
Open to their march of power.
But from that lone midnight hour
Came not back the lovely maid.

The old man tore his thin grey hair,
Mourning for his daughter fair,
And by the Holy Grail he swore
That he would make in his old age
Hard and toilsome pilgrimage
To the land of Palestine;
But there came a dream divine
To Lord Delaval's restless bed,
And angel voices sweetly said
—'Stay thou here! Thy Ada lies
Safe in the bowers of Paradise.'

And her sister Rosabel,
Rosabel of the wild grey eyes
And streaming hair of glossy brown,
Wept often by that magic well,
Ever wondering what befel
        Ada the divine;
Till tidings came that her dear Lord
Florian, the brave and true,
Had fallen upon the holy sward
On that very night of Ada's flight,
When the grass was wet with twilight dew—
Fallen by the infidel's scimitar,
As first arose the evening star.

Look thou, as thy footsteps pass
O'er the moss and leaf-strewn grass,
Into Grasmere's magic well.
In its clear depths thou shalt see
A ruby shining lucidly—

Token eternal of what befel
Fair Ada on that wondrous night,
Of vision strange and sudden flight—
Token that Heaven's most favouring breath
On the path of true love lingereth,
Even to all-embracing death.[1]

---

[1] This poem was printed in a newspaper which the editor has been unable to identify, though a cutting containing the lines has been preserved. The following note was used as a heading to the poem in the newspaper version:

'ADA OF GRASMERE

'A REMINISCENCE OF THE LATE HARTLEY COLERIDGE

'In searching through some loose papers which belonged to the late Hartley Coleridge, a long iambic poem bearing the above title has been unearthed, and, as it has in all probability not previously seen the light of day, may prove interesting. From the peculiar and unmetrical form of versification it is not readily understood by the first perusal. There is no date to determine the exact time of its composition, but, as a portion of the MS. is written on the back of the letter sheet from Wordsworth, wherein mention is made of a projected railway to the Lake District, it has evidently been in the forties.—J.W.'

INDEX TO FIRST LINES

INDEX TO FIRST LINES

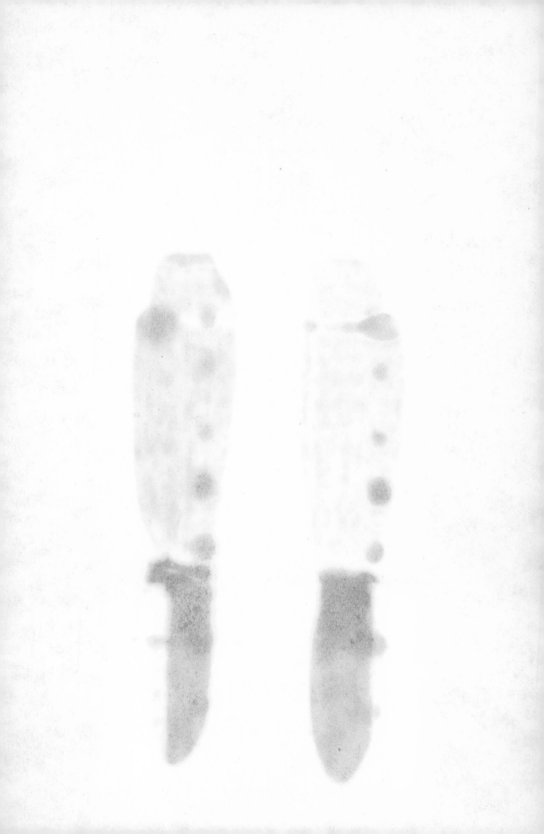

DATE DUE	

GAYLORD   PRINTED IN U.S.A.